WHAT PEOPLE ARE SAYING ABOUT

Pagan Portals – Animal Magic

Pagan Portals – Animal Magic is a multi-faceted introduction to adding animal spirits to your personal spiritual practice. So much more than just a list of animals and their meanings, this helpful little book shows the reader how to form their own unique relationship with animal spirit helpers through meditation, dance, and other meaningful activities. If you're looking for a way to add animal magic to your life, no matter what your path, this is a book you'll want on your shelf.
Laura Perry, author of *Ariadne's Thread: Awakening the Wonders of the Ancient Minoans in Our Modern Lives*

An excellent, clearly explained introduction to animal magic and it works! I read out the characteristics of my animal guide from the book and my wife said it was just like me!
Brendan Howlin, author of *The Handbook of Urban Druidry* and *Pagan Portals – The Urban Ovate*

Another great introductory book from Rachel Patterson. *Pagan Portals – Animal Magic* is packed full of information on how to find and work with animal messengers, spirit guides and familiars. The book teaches a wealth of magical techniques and is written in Rachel's delightful style. She really has a way with words as well as really knowing about her subject.
Lucya Starza, author of *Pagan Portals – Candle Magic*

T0098092

Pagan Portals
Animal Magic

Working with Spirit Animal Guides

Pagan Portals
Animal Magic

Working with Spirit Animal Guides

Rachel Patterson

Winchester, UK
Washington, USA

First published by Moon Books, 2017
Moon Books is an imprint of John Hunt Publishing Ltd., Laurel House, Station Approach,
Alresford, Hants, SO24 9JH, UK
office1@jhpbooks.net
www.johnhuntpublishing.com
www.moon-books.net

For distributor details and how to order please visit the 'Ordering' section on our website.

Text copyright: Rachel Patterson 2016

ISBN: 978 1 78535 494 6
978 1 78535 495 3 (ebook)
Library of Congress Control Number: 2016949857

All rights reserved. Except for brief quotations in critical articles or reviews, no part of this
book may be reproduced in any manner without prior written permission from the publishers.

The rights of Rachel Patterson as author have been asserted in accordance with the Copyright,
Designs and Patents Act 1988.

A CIP catalogue record for this book is available from the British Library.

Design: Stuart Davies

Printed and bound by CPI Group (UK) Ltd, Croydon, CR0 4YY, UK

We operate a distinctive and ethical publishing philosophy in all
areas of our business, from our global network of authors to
production and worldwide distribution.

CONTENTS

Who am I?

I am a witch...have been for a very long time, not the green skinned warty kind obviously...the real sort, but I am also a working wife and mother who has also been lucky enough to write and have published a book or ten. I love to learn, I love to study and have done so from books, online resources, schools and wonderful mentors over the years and still continue to learn each and every day, but have learnt the most from actually getting outside and doing it.

I am High Priestess of the Kitchen Witch Coven and an Elder at the online Kitchen Witch School of Natural Witchcraft.

My craft is a combination of old religion witchcraft, kitchen witchery, hedge witchery and folk magic. My heart is that of a Kitchen Witch. I am blessed with a wonderful husband, lovely children, a fabulous family and good friends.

I like to laugh...and eat cake...

Bibliography

Pagan Portals – Kitchen Witchcraft
Grimoire of a Kitchen Witch
Pagan Portals – Hoodoo Folk Magic
Pagan Portals – Moon Magic
A Kitchen Witch's World of Magical Plants & Herbs
A Kitchen Witch's World of Magical Foods
Pagan Portals – Meditation
The Art of Ritual
Arc of the Goddess (co-written with Tracey Roberts)
Pagan Portals – The Cailleach

Websites

My website: www.rachelpatterson.co.uk
Facebook: www.facebook.com/rachelpattersonbooks

My personal blog: www.tansyfiredragon.blogspot.co.uk
Email: tansyfiredragon@yahoo.com
www.kitchenwitchhearth.net
www.kitchenwitchuk.blogspot.co.uk
www.facebook.com/kitchenwitchuk
www.thekitchenwitchcauldron.blogspot.co.uk

My Animal Magic Journey

I love animals of all shapes and sizes and grew up in a house that always had a dog and various other pets along the way from rabbits and guinea pigs to budgerigars. Then at the age of 17 I left home to live on a farm, not just any farm, but a pig farm full of Hampshire saddleback pigs (the black ones with a pink stripe around the middle). I absolutely loved my time on the farm and felt a real connection to the pigs, which should have been a sign really because fast forward some years later and while working through a masculine energy meditation I met my lifelong animal guide – he is a wild boar and he has been with me ever since. Over the years I have picked up a few more lifelong guides in the form of a magpie, a seagull and a pigeon (bit of a bird theme). Also, while birthing my own wild stag skin shamanic drum, my drumming animal guide came to me in the form of a frog, so I have a bit of an animal farm going on, but each one is there for a reason and each one brings different strengths and wisdom to me.

Wild boar provides me with warrior spirit and courage and is also the animal that kicks my butt if I need it whereas seagull will appear when I am dealing with emotional issues and magpie comes in when magic is afoot. Pigeon, on the other hand, brings in a reminder that we need a bit of peace and quiet at times.

There are other animals of course, the ones that pop in and out from time to time and those that appear for a short while with particular messages or energies that are needed, but each one appears for a reason and it is only by paying attention that you learn from them; once you do that you will always have a connection to the animal world and it will be very rewarding.

My outlook on working with animal magic or any area of the Craft, actually even with life itself really, is to do what works for you. Trust your intuition and go with your instinct, if it feels right go with it but if it feels hinky then don't do it. And just because someone else does it one way or tells you how to do something – it doesn't necessarily make it right for you. We all walk very individual and personal pathways and what works for one doesn't always work for another. Trust your intuition because it will never let you down.

What's With all the Different Names?

There are many different names for animal guides and it depends on what tradition or pathway you follow and a lot of them seem to be interchangeable.

Totem appears to be one of the more commonly used terms although it is often associated with Native American and Aboriginal tribes, then there is animal spirit guide, messenger, companion, kindred animal, counsellor, fetch, medicine, ally and power animal to name but a few.

Interestingly enough when I looked up the word 'totem' in a dictionary to find the original meaning, I read: *'A totem is a spirit being, sacred object or symbol that serves as an emblem of a group of people such as a family, clan, lineage or tribe.'* So actually it seems that in modern paganism we have completely misappropriated the term to mean 'power animal' or 'guide'.

Spirit guide seems to be the term used mostly in shamanic practices and that makes sense to me because the animal guides are met while journeying in the spirit realm/Otherworld. But a lot of cultures believe that animals have a spirit and the term has been used all over the world.

Messengers and counsellors are general terms applied to those animals that pop in and literally give messages or deliver counsel.

Fetch is an Irish folklore term that means a spirit guide that can be in the form of a person or an animal. There are varying beliefs about the fetch. Some say that it is the true spirit of a person and appears in three forms; the fetch beast, which equates to our ideas of a totem animal; the fetch wyf, a contra-sexual spirit of the person whom it guides; and the fetch god, which is the divine face of our own fetch. The fetch in this case would be your true or lifelong familiar/totem.

Fetch can also mean a spirit doppelganger that takes on the

appearance of someone who has just died or is about to die. It isn't actually the ghost of a person, but an imitation of someone who is still alive, although folklore states that seeing a fetch is a sign that the person it portrays is about to die.

Similarly the word fylgja is from the Norse tradition and means the same as a fetch – a spirit (person or animal) who accompanies a person in connection to their fate or fortune. A Norse vitki (sorcerer) would not only draw power from his fylgja, but could also project his conscious will into it in order for it to carry out magical workings. The fylgja brought huge responsibilities and power, but could also throw hardships and challenges into the mix too. The fylgja would mould itself to the personality of the person it was attached to and the wellbeing of the human would depend on the wellbeing of the animal fylgja. Many Norse believed that the fylgja was in fact part of the hugr, or soul, and that it was capable of leaving the body and projecting itself elsewhere.

Animal medicine is another Native American term that describes the power and spirit the animal carries within. Just as you would work with plant medicine for magical purposes, animal medicine is the same; it is the essence and characteristics of the animal that can be tapped into.

Power animal is another shamanic term that refers to the idea that the spirit of animals can physically and psychologically empower us, hence the term 'power'.

Totemism

Totemism is a system of belief in which people have a mystical relationship with a spirit being such as an animal (or a plant). The spirit interacts with the group or individual and serves as their symbol. The term 'totem' derives from the Ojibwa word 'ototeman', which translates as 'one's brother-sister kin'. The Ojibwa clans traditionally emulated their animal spirits by wearing animal skins and often named their clans after animals that lived in their immediate area. Apparently the Great Spirit gifted the toodaims (totems) to the Ojibwa clan as a reminder that clan members are all related to one another.

Group totems are often based on myth or ritual and a particular animal would often become the group totem because of an event or particular moment in the past of the tribe.

Individual totemism is the relationship between a person and a particular animal they believe can grant them special power. This type of totemism is often connected with group leaders, chiefs, medicine men or shamans.

Animism

Animism is 'the attribution of a living soul to plants, inanimate objects, and natural phenomena'. The word animism is derived from the Latin word 'anima', which means 'breath' or 'soul'. It is the belief that a soul or spirit exists in every object whether it is an animal, plant or rock.

So What Term Do I Use?

When I first started working with animals and their magic I used the name totem purely because it was the most common term, but I have to admit it never really sat quite right with me. I am a witch, one that works with the old ways, so actually fetch seems to suit me much more but...this is your journey not mine so I would say go with whatever term you find more comfortable and in fact your animal may even be able to guide you with the right name for you to use. Trust your intuition, trust your animal advice. For the purpose of this book and to use a 'general' term I will work with the phrase 'animal spirit guide'.

What is Animal Magic?

Animal magic is the art of recognising and working with familiars and animal spirit guides. Animal magic shows you how to work with animals for your spiritual growth and increased magical power. Not only will an animal spirit guide give you support, wisdom and guidance, you can also draw on the power of animals to use in spell working. Mother Nature has so much to share with us through her many guises whether it is through plants, trees and herbs, the weather or via her animal kingdom – all we have to do is watch and listen. Each animal will have its own very unique characteristics, personalities and traits, but it will also have particular habitats, how it feeds, what it eats and how it raises its young, all of these things are important and can tell us something. By looking into an animal in all aspects and understanding how it fits into the scale of things – and by that I mean into the world and the eco system as a whole – we can begin to understand more about the magic that an animal spirit guide can provide us with. They can also be a reflection of our own selves or the events that are happening within our lives.

Our ancestors were far more connected with nature than we seem to be today and they understood the importance of working together with the plant and animal kingdoms; they worked in harmony with the cycles of the seasons and the ebb and flow of nature's rhythms. Priests, shamans and medicine men would wear the skins of animals and animal masks to invoke their energy and bring the power and magic of nature into being. Not that I am suggesting you throw on your leopard skin rug when you pop out to the shops, but by just being more aware of the animals and birds around you can bring about such an incredible connection.

Working with animal magic can help you find your life-long spirit guide and all that they have to offer in the form of wisdom, insight, guidance and support. Your guide can also help you understand your own true nature. Often the spirit guide that finds you is a reflection of your inner soul. Animal magic can also help you deal with the big ole outside world if you fancy a bit of shape-shifting to take on the traits of a particular animal. And it can help add extra energy and power to your spell working.

Never dismiss an animal guide if it comes to you. Not everyone will have tigers, lions or wolves, some will work very happily with an ant or a sparrow – each one has energies and messages that are right for you. Hey...I have a pigeon for goodness sake! Don't forget that the animal chooses the person...not the other way round.

Familiars

Let us start with animals that are not generally from the spirit world, but usually real flesh and blood...

Familiars are not simply the stereotypical witch's cat, although they can be cats...and they can be black. Familiars make excellent companions; they can warn you of danger, provide healing energy (physically and emotionally), and love you unconditionally. If you work magic, familiars can aid in augmenting your results with their magical and mystical powers. A familiar is a magical working companion, a creature that lends its energies to your for protection, meditational guidance, inspiration and spell casting and can provide you with a better understanding and communication with a particular species.

You can use familiars in meditations and magic; uncover superstitions about them, and draw associations with ancient deities. Learn to identify familiars with the descriptions of physical characteristics and magical attributes. Use chants to invoke an animal's greatest natural attribute. You can discover a new source of strength, wisdom and friendship in your familiar. Your familiar is your faithful friend who supports you in your magical workings. It may be a cat, dog, snake, bird or in fact anything that helps you.

Determining who or what is going to be your familiar can be one of the most difficult tasks we can face as the fur/fin/scale/feathered ones aren't always forthcoming or eager to help. Cats in particular do have a tendency to knock everything off an altar as soon as you have set it up... Remember that every animal has free will and not every animal is destined or may want to be your familiar. Just like any living being, you must ask permission and honour the answer. It is never good to rush into the decision and your familiar may end up being something you never expected. A familiar is often your pet, but can be any animal that hangs around when you are doing your magical workings.

It is best to just be patient and to just wait and watch carefully. When you are doing your workings, if your pet or a certain animal seems to have a habit of hanging around at the same place at the same time almost every time, you most probably have a little familiar.

Also remember that it is OK not to have a familiar too. I have been a witch for many, many years and although I have a whole menagerie of spirit animal guides, I don't have a familiar.

Mundane and Magical Communication
Animals communicate by body language and by voice tones. Humans have a hard time understanding what animals mean when they don't understand what the inflection of a raised tail or an ear twitch is. Mundane communication does not mean understanding words, but rather the inflections of the sounds. For example, if you come home and have had a bad day and your dog has had an accident on the floor, you may think he's acting guilty, but animals apparently do not feel guilt although to be fair some of them do look really guilty! Your dog is reacting to your body language and voice. It scares him so he tries to make you feel better – his actions and mannerisms have nothing to do with the

accident. However, I am not an animal behaviour expert so maybe they do understand to a certain extent but...remember that they aren't necessarily on the same wavelength as us.

Learning the body languages of the different species will tell you volumes. You have to separate your human side and not think like a human. Dogs are not humans, nor are cats or fish (although some of them act like it). Each creature has its own mundane language.

Magical communication will go beyond the boundaries of the mundane and can even seem like a psychic connection. For example, if you think of your pet by name and your pet comes trotting up to you, they can feel your loving energy and want to be near you. Your pet will be naturally drawn to your particular energy especially if it is positive and loving.

I have given some information about the two main animals that are usually found as familiars; the cat and the dog. Many other animals make great familiars as well such as snakes, spiders, rabbits and birds.

These are general ideas and descriptions. Remember that all animals have free will and each individual animal will have different actions they perform in order to communicate with us.

Cat

In general, purring is a sign of happiness and contentment, but it can also be an indication of pain or fear, so listen carefully to the tone of the purr and keep your eyes open for any signs of illness or injury. As we stroke our cats we are unconsciously imitating the action of a mother cat licking her kittens. As a result, the cat will often respond with kitten behaviour, such as kneading with his front paws (ouchy) as he used to knead his mother's tummy to stimulate the milk flow.

A nose-to-nose greeting from your cat is a sign that he trusts you completely. It is also a way for him to detect where you have been since he was last in contact with you (they can tell, there is no hiding it). Another sign of trust is turning on his back and allowing you to tickle his tummy.

The movement of a cat's tail is a good way of detecting his mood. Gentle swaying or flicking the end of the tail indicates a happy, sociable cat. However, if the whole of the tail flicks rapidly from side to side, your cat is not happy and may wish to be left alone. Holding the tail up stiffly in the air and fluffing it out is a sign of aggression and sometimes fear, while a tail tucked out of sight as the cat crouches to the floor and flattens his ears is an unquestionable sign of fear.

As solitary hunters, cats are very territorial and will fight quite viciously to protect their patch. Leaving scent messages is a way of marking out the boundaries and staking a claim to areas, objects or even people. With scent glands at various points on their body, including the top of their head, cats will rub against people and objects around them to leave their scent and make their property known…that's mine, this is mine, that's mine, this is mine too…

If a cat is unsure of something or someone his instinct is to get up to a higher level. Cats also think that if they can't see you then you can't see them (they are rubbish at playing hide and seek). Perhaps the most effective way to communicate with a cat is through eye contact. Never stare at a cat, just catch his eye, blink once and then look away. This is a non-threatening communication and will invite friendship and trust.

Dog

Carefully observing a pet dog can give us a glimpse into their wild, untamed and wolf side of their nature. By understanding canine thinking we can develop a much closer relationship between man (or woman) and dog, creating more of a pack dynamic rather than a master/slave kinda thing.

Dogs, like wolves, are pack animals and in the wild they will remain within their family pack for most of their entire lives.

Within the pack each animal has its own place and knows its own role. There is a strict hierarchy and feeding routine.

To our pet dogs we are the rest of their pack and their place within that pack is determined by our behaviour towards them. When I was a child we had a Springer spaniel dog who believed it was much higher up in the pack order than my younger brother; the dog would behave for my parents and myself, but would ignore any instructions from my brother because it believed he was beneath him. He found it very frustrating! Wolves hunt for their food and the success of the hunt depends on co-operation and teamwork within the pack. It is much easier for pet dogs, as their food is handed to them in a bowl on a regular schedule.

The key to a healthy and rewarding relationship with your dog is to understand pack life and how it works. Most importantly, your dog has to see you as the alpha within the pack; you need to be the top dog (pun intended). Once that role is established your dog should behave well and can be taken anywhere without any issues. Never hit a dog as punishment, they don't understand violence as a punishment and in some cases may even turn on you and I wouldn't blame them. Banishing a dog temporarily from the pack by sending him to another room for a short while is far more productive, a bit like having a dog naughty step. Dogs are uncomfortable with being banished; a wolf that is sent away from the pack in the wild has a good chance of dying of starvation or being killed by another pack. Dogs remember this kind of imprint. When he returns from solitary don't pay him any attention for a while, this is how a mother dog would treat an unruly puppy.

Rolling over on to their back is a sign of submission in dogs and an indication that they view you as a higher member of the pack. By the same token dogs who are snappish with children view them as lower pack members – they think of them as puppies who need to be put in their place by older dogs.

Begging for food from the table is another indication that your dog sees you as a higher pack member and he will wait patiently with his eyes fixed on you until he discovers whether or not you have left him any scraps. This is classic pack behaviour and stems from the strict feeding hierarchy that wolves have. I have never done this with any of our pet dogs, I don't like them begging at the table and they have always been taught to lie underneath the table when we eat, but that is a personal decision.

When a dog licks your face it is harking back to puppy behaviour as wolf puppies will lick the muzzle of a parent or older wolf to persuade them to regurgitate food – you probably don't need to go quite that far... This also explains why domestic dogs have been known to eat vomit...ewww. To the dog, however, this is just another way of exhibiting natural pack behaviour.

Animal Spirit Guides

And now to the world of animal spirits...

Animal spirit guides are those animals that you have had an affinity for or have seemed to have walked with you for a very long period of time. They may have walked with you for many lifetimes, many years or just have recently came into focus as you have had need of them. Your spirit guide animal need not be limited to animals on this planet at this time, as mythical creatures and extinct ones are useful guides too.

There are several types of animal spirit guides that you may encounter, these are the main ones:

Lifelong: This is the animal spirit guide that you will have throughout your entire life. It may appear to you at any time during your life span, but once it is with you it will stay for the rest of your existence. This animal may be one you have had an affinity with or have appeared at various points. This creature may have in fact been with you for many lifetimes.

Journey: This animal walks with you for a length of time, which could be weeks or years or any period of time within. It is a guide that keeps you on your pathway. These animals can come around quickly as you need their help during certain times in your life and then leave just as quickly. They may linger as long as the blink of an eye or for many months. These usually appear when you have a journey to start and will stay with you until that particular life experience is completed.

Message: This animal sporadically just pops into your life on a moment-by-moment basis. It may show up one day as a 'wait a minute' moment, to let you know something is going on. Take note of the animal and what message it is trying to impart to you.

Shadow: This is your side that you may fear the most. Once you conquer the fear of this animal it becomes one of your greatest strengths. This spirit guide reflects the part within yourself that you are least confident about or the bit of your personality you dislike the most.

Purpose: This guide will show up for particular events, rituals or journeys. I have a black panther animal spirit guide that only comes to me when I am hedge riding (journeying) to the underworld. My wild boar guide refuses to travel to the underworld so the panther arrives to accompany me instead. The same happens with my frog spirit guide, he is only with me when I am drumming.

Animal Medicine

By observing animals in natural surroundings and their associated behaviours, we begin to get glimpses of each creature's medicine. This understanding in turn helps us to connect with the animal spirit, honour it and utilise the magic within our own lives and spell work.

Our spirit animal and its medicine can help us in various ways:

- It can give the strength, energy and enthusiasm to face up to difficult situations or challenges in your life.
- It can shed some light on an important decision you may have to make.
- It can offer ideas for a particular project and find solutions for situations that seem unclear.
- It can help to access your inner strengths.
- It can help to overcome your fears.
- It can unleash your hidden potential and true qualities.
- It can build up your resistance to illness.
- It can speed up the healing process when you are ill.
- It can help you to discover important information in special circumstances.
- It can help you find lost objects.
- It can keep you out of harm and help you avoid dangerous or life-threatening situations.
- It can help protect you from physical, mental or emotional pain.
- It can comfort you when the things are tough.
- It can help you to improve your relationships.
- It can help you to develop your self confidence.
- It can guide your spiritual journey.

The Roles of a Spirit Animal Guide

Counsellor and Messenger: In this role your spirit animal helps you to understand situations and offers answers and guidance, it can give you options to help with decisions or choices. Your animal spirit guide can give an indication of which pathway should be taken and what behaviour to adopt.
Protector: In this role your spirit animal guide can lend you the strength, courage and energy to face anything that is thrown at you. It can also warn when danger is approaching or when a situation is about to turn sour. Each animal will

react differently to scenarios so it is important to listen very carefully to what they are trying to tell you. Different animals will have specific reactions to danger.

Teacher: Your animal spirit guide can be a great teacher and show you how to use your own energy and inner spirit to its full potential throughout your life. The animals that appear regularly can give us important messages and they will continue to appear until we have learnt and acted upon the lesson.

Healer: Animal spirit guides are excellent healers and can show us not only how to heal our own emotional, physical and spiritual ailments, but also how to heal others. Your animal spirit guide will lend you healing energy. It can also show you the best treatment or technique to use and help speed up the healing process.

Guide: Your animal spirit guide is all the above roles in one neat package. Your lifelong guide will be all of these things and more. Once you have found your guide your life will change forever, for the better, and you will wonder how you ever got along without it.

Meditations and Spells to Find Familiars and Animal Spirit Guides

There are many ways in which you can meet your spirit animal. In general we have a main spirit animal that stays with us throughout our lives. Sometimes another spirit animal will appear depending on the lessons we need to take on board at different times in our lives. It is also possible for other animal messengers or allies to appear to help us with a particular task. With a measure of meditation and observation, when we are listening to our intuition we can start to recognise our spirit animal and our other animal allies.

Techniques include meditations, dreams, dancing, drumming, spells or just being particularly drawn to one animal or seeing images of it in everyday life.

Have you always been fascinated by a particular animal or has a specific animal appeared continuously in your life? Do you see any animals on a regular basis whether it is on the walk or drive to work or even on the television? And of course...are you frightened of any animals? Sometimes the animal we fear is the one we can learn the most from, this would be your shadow animal spirit.

Given below are some exercises to help you determine your own main personal spirit animal.

The Animal to Which You Feel Most Drawn

Is there an animal to which you have always been drawn? Do you collect miniatures, ornaments or cuddly toy versions of a specific animal? Was there an animal that you particularly liked when you were a child, the thought of which still draws you? Do you live with a cat, a dog, snake or a horse to which you have a deep attachment? Has a close relative or good friend mentioned a specific type of animal; does this animal frequently cross your path? Is there an animal that keeps showing up at difficult times in your life? Or is there an animal that just seems to hang around you?

You may already have made a connection with your animal spirit guide, but not be consciously aware of it. It may be working its magic and making a link with you in preparation for you discovering it!

If you are scared of a particular animal and you are able to overcome these fears you will then have an excellent connection with it. If you have been bitten by an animal the Native Americans would say that it is testing you to discover your strength and that you are probably already in possession of its medicine, bit of an extreme method though!

In order to discover our spirit animal it is really important to stay open and to observe the animals that appear in our lives. Bill boards, TV shows, newspaper articles, labels on cartons – signs could be anywhere…

Dreams

Any meetings with animals in dreams should be taken as seriously as any unexpected encounter in our day-to-day lives. Your spirit animal can easily appear to you in a dream; we have no geographical limits and can meet up with an animal whom we wouldn't ordinarily meet. My own animal guides are all fairly 'every day' and the birds in particular arrive in my garden (the wild boar is a bit more elusive), but I have worked with other more exotic animals. A distinguishing mark of a spirit animal is the fact that it appears with unfailing regularity. One of the advantages to discovering your spirit animal in a dream is that it's easier to discover its qualities and its medicine by deciphering and reflecting on the circumstances and the way it appeared to you in your dream.

This method usually works very well for me:

Before you go to sleep, hold a glass of water between your hands, charging the water and asking your spirit animal to appear in your dreams. Drink the water just before settling down to sleep, telling yourself that you will remember the dream where your spirit animal appears.

Leave a notepad and pen by the bed so that you can write down what happened in your dream upon waking, before you forget it!

Observing Auras and Behaviours of your Animal Spirit Guide

When a spirit animal is close to someone their energies can mingle together. The person will tend to take on the qualities, the movements and even the behaviour of that particular animal; not literally – they don't start digging holes in the floor or roaring thankfully – these signs are subtle. When we are speaking we often use analogies with particular animals in mind. For example; beavering away, busy as a bee, slinky like a cat, proud as a peacock, fierce as a lion, stubborn as a mule, strong as an ox, sly as a fox and quiet and timid as a mouse, to name but a few. We often refer to people's qualities and relate them to animal attributes. For instance someone may have feline grace, be bearlike or birdlike and twitchy, have hawk eyes or puppy dog eyes. Some people even start to walk like their spirit animals, striding, skipping, prancing, shuffling, hesitating or sneaking along silently... I have tried flying, it doesn't work...

By being aware of how we move around and how we act, we can often work out which is our spirit animal. Now and then a person's aura will take on the form of his or her animal. This aura can extend all around the person and it is sometimes possible to see an animal taking shape. You can try looking at your own aura in a mirror. If you focus your eyes on a point just beyond your head and bring your peripheral vision forward allowing your eyesight to unfocus you can sometimes see your aura extending outward from your physical body. If you are lucky your spirit animal guide may also appear. Ask your friends and family for their observations on how you move and behave or if they perceive any particular animal traits that you might have.

Meditation

Meditation is an excellent tool enabling you to meet an animal spirit guide and is my personal favourite method. It allows you to meet not only spirit animal guides, but also to obtain messages and snippets of wisdom. You might meet different animals along the way or it may lead you to your lifelong guide; be open to whatever comes your way.

This is a meditation that will hopefully enable you to discover your animal guide or messenger:

Make yourself comfortable in a place where you won't be disturbed.

Close your eyes and start to focus on your breathing, deep breaths in and deep breaths out…

As your world around you dissipates you find yourself standing on a dirt track crossroads in the middle of a forest.

The pathway ahead of you leads further into the forest and is darker and full of dense lush foliage, it is not scary or frightening though.

You turn and look at the pathway to your left, this one seems to widen out and looks like it leads down to the ocean or a large lake because you can see the glint of blue waters in the distance.

You turn again and the pathway behind you appears to lead out of the forest and upwards into a mountain range, the pathway looks clear and easy to follow as it winds up the side of a hill.

And to your right the forest clears to show a pathway leading onto dry desert sand with just a few rocks scattered around.

Which pathway are you drawn to take? Perhaps you would like to investigate all of them in turn?

Take your time and walk slowly down the first pathway that you are drawn to. Once there, sit down and wait, what can you see? What can you hear? What can you smell? Take a while to explore your surroundings.

Then see what animal, beast or bird greets you. Spend some time with it and find out what it would like to help you with.

You may only wish to walk one pathway. If so, once you are finished thank the animal and make your way back to the centre of the crossroads and come back to this reality.

If you want to explore more come back to the centre of the cross-roads and take a different pathway…

Once you are ready, again come back to the centre.

When you are finished completely, slowly bring yourself back to this reality, opening your eyes and wriggling your fingers and toes.

You can come back to this meditation spot any time or as many times as you want to or feel the need to.

Spell

If working magic is your thing then you can create a spell to find your animal spirit guide. How you do it is up to you – use your intuition to see what you can come up with, but here are some suggestions to get you started:

- Light a candle and watch the flame burn. As it does so, ask out loud what animal is your spirit guide – keep watching the flame and see what images appear. This would also work with flames from a fire.
- Scrying – put some water into a bowl that has a dark interior, drop a silver coin into the bottom and ask what animal your spirit guide is…watch the surface of the water for any images.
- Write your petition on a slip of paper, asking what your animal spirit guide is and light it from a candle flame. Allow it to burn safely then throw the ashes to the winds,

bury them in the earth or drop them into running water. Keep an eye on your dreams or signs around you over the next few days.

- If you like to work with the power of the moon then stand outside during a full moon and ask her for guidance to find your animal spirit guide. Keep an eye on your dreams or signs around you over the next few days.

- If you prefer to work with the sun then you could write your petition on a leaf, perhaps just the words 'animal guide', and leave it out in the full sun to dry and again watch for animals in your dreams or signs and symbols as you go about your daily routine.

Dancing with Your Spirit Animal

Dancing is a fun and energetic way to make contact with the animal spirit world and is easy-peasy to do, especially if you have a drum or a rattle to use, if you don't you can clap your hands or click your fingers instead. Although a drum could be as simple as an old biscuit tin that you beat with your hand.

Start by creating a beat with your rattle, drum or hands, keep the beat quite quick.

Turn to the four directions in turn and call to the animals that correspond to them.

Start with the east and call to the animals of the element of air – the birds and the winged allies of your choice – the eagle, the owl and the dove.

Then turn to the south and call to the animals vibrating with the element of fire such as the snake, the lizard and the phoenix.

Turn to the direction of the west and call to the water animals such as the dolphin, the whale and the salmon.

Finally, turn to face the north and call to the animals from the earth element – the bear, the deer and the horse.

Once you have gone through the list of animals of the four

directions, get down on the ground, all the time keeping a beat, and call to the spirits of the land and below.

Then stand on the tips of your toes, look up toward the sky, and call the spirits of the skies and above.

Carry on beating out the rhythm and start to dance. Let your body be filled with the energy that comes in. Let yourself go and dance even if the movements seem strange; it is OK, no one is watching you! Be free, be inspired, and be wild! Invite the spirits of the animals to join you and ask your spirit animal to direct the movements of your body. After a while you may feel the presence of a particular animal and you will have the feeling that your body is taking on its qualities, its attitude and its body language.

Once you have made that animal connection and you really feel it is there, keep the beat going, but talk to the animal.

When you are ready you can start to slow the beat down and calm your dancing down gradually until you come to a gentle stop. Thank the animal for its energy and ground yourself.

Invoking Your Spirit Animal With a Rattle or Drum

One of the oldest techniques for meeting your spirit animal and one used by our ancestors for generations is to work with the beat of a drum or a rattle.

Our ancestors used the rhythm and power of the sound of instruments to send their deepest wishes to the spirit world. You can use a drum or a rattle, but any musical instrument would work well. The important thing is the strength of your intent to draw an animal to you.

The technical bit of this is that the rhythm used consists of a regular beat (around three beats per second). This regular beat enables your brainwaves to go from beta to alpha and then theta – the waves at which the brain vibrates during dreams.

When you allow yourself to be immersed in the beat it enables you to drift to a deeper consciousness, something like daydreaming. It will make it easier for your animal spirit guide to make a connection.

Make yourself comfortable in a darkened room and light a candle or if possible do this outside around a camp fire (I know that isn't always a feasible plan!) You could also burn magical herb blends or incense to add to the atmosphere.

Sit down on the floor in front of the candle or the fire and start to beat your drum, shake your rattle, ring your bell (or whatever instrument you have chosen to use) to a regular beat, failing that just clap your hands.

Keep your eyes half closed and call to your spirit animal. Clear your mind and be open...

Allow the images and sounds of any animals that might appear to float through your mind unhindered. You might get flashes of images or you might get more prominent ones, just allow them to flow.

Continue to create your beat for about 20-15 minutes. After this time, you should hopefully have an idea or a hint of a particular animal. It may come to you suddenly or you may just feel a particular energy beside you.

The best way to find out if it is your spirit animal guide is to ask it...pay attention to the reply and listen very carefully to what it has to say. It may not speak at all, it might just give you a sign instead, but it will hopefully be a clear one that makes perfect sense to you.

Once you have met your animal continue the beat while concentrating on the energy of the animal, feel its strength.

When you are ready thank the animal and gradually slow the beat to a stop. Don't forget to ground yourself afterwards, perhaps by having something to eat and drink.

Ritual

If working in ritual is more your thing then you can design one with the intent of meeting your animal spirit guide. Create an altar with representations of different animals on or any other items you feel drawn to place on it, whether it is candles, crystals or natural things such as twigs and leaves, to make a connection with nature.

Cast your circle perhaps using a chant that invokes basic animal energy maybe even include some drumming. Something like:

I cast this circle round and round
To call upon my animal spirit guide to be found
This circle brings protection in
And protection round about

OK, I am not a poet, but you get the idea.

Call in the quarters and with this you could call upon animals that represent each element. (See the chapter on animals in ritual for more details). If you want to invite deity to join you then maybe pick gods and goddesses that are associated with animals. Place an offering on your altar and call to your animal spirit guide. Sit quietly or drum so that you enter a meditative state where hopefully you will meet your animal guide. Don't forget to thank your guide and deity afterwards and release the quarters.

A Journey or Over the Hedge
As a Hedge Witch when I go on a journey I 'hedge ride', which is very similar to the shamanic journeying that is also sometimes referred to as pathworking or vision questing. It is an ideal exercise to bring healing and work with my inner self. I always have a particular spirit animal guide for my hedge riding – my black panther comes with me. But a journey is a brilliant way to meet your animal spirit guide too. It is something that you should only work with once you are experienced with meditation and know what you are doing because essentially you are travelling to the Otherworld.

A journey is a structured meditation with a purpose to it, a

guided pathworking into the Otherworld or onto other planes.
The basics:

- Why are you journeying? Well in this case it would be to meet your spirit animal guide.
- What path will you take and what is your destination? Decide on this before you start.
- What would you like to encounter? This would be your animal guide.
- What image do you want to use to take you from this world onto your journey? For example, it could be a gate, a doorway, a hole in the ground or a hole in a tree.

Once you have made these decisions you need a framework, starting with an induction, which is where you enter the journey, the trance-like state you will be in. There the body of the journey is the purpose, in this case to find your animal spirit guide. And then the closure, where you specify a place that allows you to leave and come back to reality; set this before you start.

It helps to write down your framework or even record it onto your phone or laptop, but go with what works for you. Your journey will take unexpected twists and turns, but it needs the structure in place to work properly.

The basic steps for path working are very similar to those of meditation.

Find a safe, quiet and comfortable place. Make sure you won't be disturbed.

Ground and centre, perhaps by taking a few deep breaths and stilling your mind.

Turn on your recording or just close your eyes to begin your journey. Visualise your induction point, the entry to your journey. Just listening or visualising your induction should take you into your trance state, but if it doesn't, focus on your breathing to obtain a meditative state.

Visualise your induction, see yourself at the entry. Take a moment to fix that place in your mind. See yourself reaching out to touch the entry way, feel how real it is, notice all the details, the feel, any sounds, any smells.

Once you have the entry point in your mind solidly you can begin your journey.

Walk through the gateway entering the body of your journey, notice all the details – listen, touch, smell, hear, taste, and take note of everything. Set the details in your mind so that you will recall them when you come back to reality. Sometimes even the smallest detail may be important.

If you meet anyone on your pathworking, whether it is a human, a deity, a fae, an animal, whatever, please be polite and respectful. Don't touch any animal or being without asking first. If you are asked to move on then do so with respect. These beings work on a different plane, you do not want to upset them. Do not take anything unless you know it has actually been given to you. Use your common sense and mind your manners!

When you have finished your pathworking return to the point you started at. Go back to your gateway and go through, but do so slowly, coming back to reality slowly and calmly. And always ground afterwards – which can be done by having something to eat and drink.

Empty Nest...or Pen...or Paddock

What happens if you end up doing all of the exercises, meditations, spells and dancing about like a loony and you are still Billy No Mates? Patience...yup. Sorry, I know it sucks, but be patient. There are several reasons why it might be taking some time, it could be that your spirit animal guide is a bit sassy (i.e. a total git) and is making you work really hard for it or it could be that the time just isn't right for you at the moment. Seriously I know it is hard, but patience is the key. Try again later and remain open to whatever signs or signals the animal might tease you with. The fact that you have picked up this book, hopefully read it and worked with some of the ideas given means that you have made the first step; your animal guide is there it may just be biding its time to meet you.

What Does it Mean?

So you have an animal spirit guide – but what does it mean? Each spirit guide will be with you for a reason, what you need to work out and understand is why it is with you.

Say a butterfly came to you – the butterfly symbolises reincarnation, magic, beauty and love and transformation of the personality and life. Understanding where you are in the cycle of your life and using it to the fullest. It also covers divination concerning future events that have a bearing on your cycle of life and rebirth. Relate that to your own life and situation and learn from it. The butterfly is with you to help you, assist you and guide you.

Or maybe a griffin has joined you – seeing a griffin is a sign of powerful new beginnings of learning how to use psychic skills in a useful manner. But on the negative it is subconscious punishment for love of riches, greed or of desiring riches. Its magical attributes understand the relationship between psychic energy and cosmic forces along with spiritual wisdom and enlightenment. It brings the dark side of ourselves into submission.

What about an otter? His magical attributes are finding inner treasures or talents, faithfulness, gaining wisdom, and the ability to recover from a crisis. Be sensible, but not overly suspicious, when something or someone new enters your life. Its appearance points to a need to enjoy life rather than just endure it. Social life, friends, happiness, guidance to uncovering talents, psychic or physical, all these things relate to the otter.

All the animals have their own unique powers and can all be utilised and called upon to assist us when we need them.

What Next?
So, once you have your familiar and/or spirit guide is that it? Nope! Everything that is worth having takes a bit of work to

keep. You need to honour your guides and make sure you stay connected with them. Apart from learning all about them as I mentioned before, you do need to reaffirm your connection regularly, they need attention!

Make pictures of them, even if your art isn't that good. Print images from the internet or look into charity shops/thrift stores for statues and images of them.

Create an altar to honour them.

Donate to wildlife charities if you have some spare cash, even small change will help.

Make charms and amulets for your familiars' and pets' collars.

Research your animal. Work to understand it. Where does it live? What does it eat? How does it act, walk, hunt, and look after its young? Read as much about them as possible.

You can expand that to cover what element it corresponds to, how it defends itself and so on; does it have its own legends or folklore?

Don't ignore your spirit guides in your daily life. Take them out with you when you go anywhere, say good morning to a picture of your animal each day, put a statue on your altar, and wear a pendant representing your particular animal. You need to communicate with your guide and create a relationship.

In order to form a strong bond with your guide, familiar or totem, mutual respect is essential. You must listen to your guide's point of view and suggestions.

All these things will help you to understand your animal more and why it found you. Remember that there will be positive AND negative characteristics to any animal.

Working with animal magic takes time and effort, but can be very rewarding and enlightening.

Animal familiars and spirit guides are there to help you on your life walk. They are brothers and sisters to us all and coexist with us on this earth. We share many paths with them and sometimes don't even know it! Learning from these animals can be a lifetime experience, even many lifetimes, and sometimes the animals may not even be ones that we know today.

Solitary or a Pack?

How many spirit animal guides can you have? The answer is more than one, although it seems that one will usually stand out among the others as your 'main' guide, you may have others that reoccur regularly and if you work with the spirit guide medicine pentacle exercise below you will end up with nine!

How do you know if an animal is your spirit guide? An animal guide is usually that animal that you have had an affinity with for a long time. Your animal guide is always by your side no matter what. But the easiest way to check is to ask it...

Can your spirit guide be an extinct or a mythological creature? The answer is yes it can, but realise the fact that information on these creatures may or may not be forthcoming, and you do have to take the negative along with the positive as with all the others as well. We also step into dragon territory here, which is a huge subject as dragons come in all shapes, sizes and forms, but they too can make excellent animal spirit guides (although you might want to avoid the chaos dragon). I had a student once who worked very well with a Tyrannosaurus rex animal spirit guide; it was incredibly strong and powerful although it had a bit of a temper...

Remember that animals have free will, and your animal spirit guide will come to you when you are in need of it, and only when you are ready.

Find Information on your Spirit Guide Animal

Before you rush headlong all excited because you have found a spirit guide animal you need to learn all you can about it. You wouldn't get in a car and switch everything on if you didn't know how to drive would you? (Well I would hope not anyway.) Take your time and do your homework first. Find out all you need to know first then you can start working with your animal.

Now Ask Questions

Start with the basics such as where does it like to live? Is it an earthy creature or does it nest high in trees or maybe it swims in the ocean? All these habitats are very different and will affect the spiritual energy and how you connect with it. What are the animal's characteristics? Is it predator or prey? What are its good points and bad points? How does it interact with other animals or its young? What is its physical presence? How will all of these things affect how you work and connect with it?

What element does it correspond to?

Air (creatures that fly): Most birds, flying fish, butterfly, dragonfly, ladybird, bee and insects.

Fire (creatures that creep): Scorpion, lion, lizard, horse, desert creatures and those that sting.

Water (creatures that swim): Fish, seahorse, dolphin, seal, walrus, crab, seagull, whale, duck, beaver.

Earth (creatures that walk): Rabbit, cow, wolf, bear, deer, mole, ferret, mouse and forest or field dwelling creatures.

Don't be final with these definitions, however. They are meant as a tool to learn from, not as a box to file them in. Many animals correspond to more than one element. Dolphin is water because it lives in the sea, but it also jumps beautifully into the air. Duck swims on the water, but also flies in the air. Snake slithers in the desert, but also has a powerful bite so I would class it as both earth and fire. What does this teach you about the creature?

Where Does it Live?

Perched high on a mountain cliff, the goat is very different from a water-loving hippopotamus. While goat might teach about sure-footedness on your path or seeking new heights, hippo is more likely to tell you to remain grounded, but with its water connection it will ask you to watch your emotions too.

What is its 'Cycle of Power'?

Bat is active at night, the rooster crows at dawn, stag turns to rut in the autumn and the snow owl brings winter with her. The power cycle of your animal spirit guide will show you times when you will have more access to energy.

What Does it Look Like?

In magic, the Law of Signatures states that 'the attributes without, mirror the qualities within'. Not that I am suggesting you will end up looking like your animal guide, I hope not anyway...I really don't want to look like a wild boar but...take a look just in case there are some qualities that mirror your own.

What Do the Shape and Colour of your Animal Guide Suggest?

The lion or golden eagle suggest solar powers while the jaguar and owl are nocturnal and lunar. The colour of plumage on a bird may connect with the chakras or the white of a swan's feathers may suggest peace.

How Does it Defend Itself?

Does it roll over and hide as a way of defence such as the opossum or stick its head in the sand like ostrich? Or does it stand and fight or even charge at its enemies like the wild boar? These will show you how your animal deals with conflict and arguments and will reflect the energies it can lend to you.

Note: The ostrich doesn't actually bury its head in the sand, it wouldn't be able to breathe. What this bird actually does is dig a hole for her eggs, she regularly puts her head into the hole to turn the eggs...don't believe everything you read or see!

What Does it Eat and How Does it Hunt for Food?

Bear this in mind when you are working with shape-shifting especially. If you are vegan or vegetarian you probably don't want to shape-shift into a meat-eating tiger...

But what an animal eats and how it hunts will also show you more insights into your own way of life.

What are its Mating Habits and How Does it Raise its Young?

Does your animal mate for life or is it a bit of a gigolo? Is it a gentleman or lady on the mating scene or a big show off like the peacock? Does it have to fight with other males or females for the attention of a mate? And then how does it look after its young? Does it stay in a family pack like jackals or is it known for eating its young like sharks have a tendency to do...

What Sounds Does it Make?

Is your animal the quiet silent type or does it laugh loudly like a hyena? The whale sings a soulful song whereas birds tend to chirp happily, this is all important to learn about.

What Animal Family Does your Animal Guide Belong To?

Study its close relatives and see what they have in common. Most animals come from a larger group and studying the others that it is related to can offer interesting insights.

What Can I Learn From Mythology and Folklore?

Myths, fairy tales and folk stories often highlight the link between people and animals. They offer a bit of wisdom and guidance woven into the stories and bring the magical and spiritual connection to animals.

What about the princess who kisses the frog? He becomes a handsome prince and she lives happily ever after (or so we are told). This story is about transformations and that is one of the characteristics of working with frog as an animal spirit guide.

Many myths tell of gods that take on animal forms. The ancient Egyptian gods are often portrayed with animal heads such as the cat headed goddess Bast and Horus with his hawk head. Animals are also included in creation myths and stories telling how they helped to create worlds.

They also appear in stories highlighting their main personalities so the lion would be brave and courageous, but the fox would be sly and the dog would be a loyal friend. My own wild boar is seen in many stories symbolising war.

These stories all have powerful meanings and lessons to teach.

Look at Both Positive and Negative

Every animal will have both positive and negative properties, energy and characteristics. Your animal spirit guide is with you to teach you and help you grow. They have a huge amount of insight and advice so pay attention to what they bring to you. Be open...

But remember...look at their negative side as well as the positive, it may teach you even more about yourself.

Seeking Animal Wisdom

So you have a new friend and you have the basics, but what happens next? I suggest it is time to really get to know your new ally. So, get yourself a blank sheet of paper and pen or a new document up on the computer screen ready...

Let me use my wild boar as an example, you would obviously use the animal that came to you. I have only covered question to show you how it works, but use the checklist below for your spirit animal guide and answer each one, it really will give you a detailed overview of the animal and why it is with you.

First I look at its habit and how it lives: woodland, marshland and agricultural land. Generally sedentary animals, they like to stay within their home range, they don't migrate. Females spend more time in dense, safe habits than the males do. They breed seasonally and during that time the usually solitary males move into female groups and fight rival males for dominance. They prefer to live in small social groups and have a matriarchal group with usually two or three mature females including their most recent litters. Different female groups will co-exist in the same areas, but they keep their social identity. They are primarily nocturnal although they may venture out during the day for food. Mostly the days are spent sleeping up to 12 hours a day followed by a short period of grooming on awakening then four to eight hours of feeding during the night. Wild boar have very poor eyesight.

So, what can I learn from wild boar?

They like to feel safe and love the comfort of their own home. The females like to keep in girly groups and spend a lot of their time looking after the babies. They love their sleep and they like to eat…

Those are characteristics. How do they apply to me?

Sounds just like me – 12 hours of sleep and eight hours of eating – perfect…

To me this echoes the safety and comfort that I feel when I am at home, it is my sanctuary, but it is also a reminder that it is good to get out with friends every so often and have a girly chat. Sleep is important and this also reiterates the need to get a proper balance between work and rest. It is also about motherhood and taking care of family.

Your Totem Animal Checklist

- Where does the animal live and how does it interact with the habitat?
- How might this animal's habitat affect its spiritual energy for animal magic?
- What are the animal's natural aptitudes, demeanours, and characteristics and how might those affect your magic for

good or bad?

- How does this creature interact with other creatures?
- Who is predator and who is prey?
- How might this animal's physical structure and natural behaviours influence its symbolic value in spell craft and other magical processes?
- What element does it correspond to? Consider the combination of elements too. What does this teach you about the creature?
- Where does it live?
- What is its 'cycle of power'?
- What does it look like?
- What does the shape, colour, etc, of your animal suggest?
- How does it defend itself?
- What does it eat and how does it hunt for food?
- What are its mating habits and how does it raise its young? What sounds does it make?
- What animal family does your spirit guide belong to?
- What can you learn from mythology and folklore?
- What can you learn from your spirit guide animal?

Shape-Shifting

Shape-shifting is a change, a way to help us become better by becoming different than we usually are. We already shape-shift everyday in many different ways, we often put on different 'faces' to everyone we meet. We are a different person to our boss, to our co-worker, a stranger, a spouse, to our children. Our ancestors shifted to go on spiritual quests to learn answers about themselves and the world around them.

Shape-shifting can bring you closer to your animal spirit guide or it can help you to take on the characteristics of a particular animal.

Practical and Mystical Aspects of Shape-Shifting

- Relating to others around you and adjusting your behaviour as conditions require.
- Being able to be gentle or strong, whatever is needed at the time.
- Teaching self discipline to achieve your goals.
- Adapting to changes around you.
- Turning your mood around from dark to light.
- Discovering your inner talents.
- Finding your blockages and self-imposed limitations and overcoming them.
- Banishing hurt, pain and negative feelings.
- Letting go of the past.
- Developing new skills.
- Strengthening your talents and skills.
- Strengthening your aura.
- Improving your lucid dreaming and astral travel skills.
- Healing.
- Gaining knowledge.
- Finding answers.

- Connecting to nature.
- Psychic protection.
- Aligning with your spirit animal guide.
- Gaining flexibility towards life lessons.

Do not decide to do this type of exercise lightly. You can be overwhelmed by the experience. For example, if you haven't done your mundane research and are a vegetarian and decide to shape-shift into a carnivorous animal, it may be a very disturbing experience on many levels. If you are a peaceful person by nature who has trouble dealing with authority and you are really sensitive, then leaping straight into the guise of a lion could be very traumatic. Be prepared.

Shape-shifting brings us many gifts. We acquire many different aspects that help us in the world, practical and mystical. We acquire also the best of the animals that we have chosen too, but also we have to be careful because we will acquire the negative as well. Remember the female and male in any species can be extremely different in characteristics so study your animals carefully.

Shape-Shifting Visualisation

Make yourself comfortable somewhere that you won't be disturbed. If you like you can burn some incense and pop some quiet plinky plonky music on in the background.

Close your eyes and start to focus on your breathing, deep breathes in and deep breathes out...allow your body to completely relax.

As your world around you dissipates you find yourself in a beautiful forest, the sun is shining and dappled light is shining down between a canopy of leaves. Ahead of you is a pathway so you start to walk...listen to the sounds of the forest as you start to move...

The track leads you to a clearing with a large standing stone right in the centre, so you make your way towards it.

Once you are in front of the standing stone, which towers above you, you put your hand out to touch it. As your hand meets the cold hard rock it shimmers and a swirling pattern of mist appears on the face of the rock. The mist starts to clear and the whole face of the rock turns into a reflective mirrored surface.

You can see your image reflecting back at you, but then it starts to blur and in place of your reflection appears an animal standing gazing at you. This animal has something to teach you, it has a lesson and/or a message for a part of your life right now.

Feeling totally comfortable and at ease you step into the mirror image...

Allow yourself to become the animal...make the connection and begin the transformation piece by piece...

Once you are fully transformed into the animal, move around, run, jump, hop, fly – whatever the animal would usually do. How does it feel? What view of the world do you have now that you are in your animal shape? Take as much time as you need...

When you are ready, head back to the mirror stone and slowly and gently shape-shift back into your human form. Thank the animal for its help and support.

Step back through the mirror stone...

Walk back to the track and head to the edge of the woods coming back to reality with each footstep that you take.

Open your eyes and wriggle your fingers and toes and make a note of any messages, thoughts or experiences.

Animal Guide Pentacle/Medicine Wheel

Many Native American tribes use the medicine wheel and most of them use animal totems within it. Teachings and methods will vary from tribe to tribe, but essentially they all work with nature and the teachings that it has to offer; each part of creation has a particular place in the 'great medicine wheel of life'.

Animal medicine in the Native American way refers to the connection of the Great Mystery and to all of life that also includes healing of the mind, body and spirit, bringing you personal power, strength and understanding. It is the living of life in such a way that brings healing to Mother Earth and to all the creatures that live on her. It is 'all encompassing' and entails walking on the planet in perfect harmony with her energies, the seasons and the animals and plants on her.

I have worked with a medicine wheel system for years that involves nine totem animals, each one having its own special place, energies and position on the medicine wheel, but because of my own particular pathway, that of a Witch, it was suggested to me by a very wise lady that I create something more 'witchy' so my animal spirit medicine pentacle was born. The animals will represent, assist, support and help each individual person, their abilities, talents and challenges.

There are seven directions surrounding our bodies; East, South, West, North, Above, Below and Within. You will have an animal spirit guide for each of these directions and each one will have different lessons for you relevant to that direction. The other two animals that make up the nine guides are the ones that walk beside you at all times, they correspond to your right side and your left side.

You may only need to find these animals once; they will then always be YOUR animals for your own personal medicine wheel...but life changes and so do you so be flexible.

Pentacle Medicine Wheel

Above: Honouring the divine, you are connected and part of the 'all'. This animal teaches you how to honour and guides you to other worlds and dimensions.
Below: How to stay grounded and on your path. This animal will teach you how to stay grounded and centred and how to

make a true connection to Mother Earth.

Within: How to be true to yourself. This animal will guide you to your inner truth and show you how to be happy and content. It also guards your own very special inner sacred space.

Left: Your feminine energy, trust, receiving and nurturing. This animal shows you how to receive the abundance you deserve and to nurture yourself and others. This animal is your teacher.

Right: Your masculine energy, courage and warrior spirit. This animal is your guardian and protector.

Earth: Silent, centred, inner work, stability, home and hearth, manifesting and confidence. This animal gives you wisdom and counsel and also prompts you when the time is right to speak and when to listen.

Air: To know, intuition, intellect, wisdom and imagination. This animal guides you to your spiritual challenges and shows you the way to enlightenment.

Fire: To will, discipline, application, focus and determination. This animal brings protection, but also helps you to know when to trust, it also releases your passion and inner child.

Water: To dare, emotions, challenges, conviction and following your heart. This animal leads you to your personal truth and the answers that lie within, it can also help guide you to your goals.

The medicine pentacle is used to gather together the energies of all the animals, creatures, beings, humans, Mother Earth, Father Sky and all our relations in the universe.

The medicine pentacle is a symbol for the cycle of life, which is forever evolving and brings us new lessons and truths as we walk along our own individual pathways and journeys. Walking the pentacle means that every direction is to be honoured and experienced and the circle that encompasses them all must also be walked.

The medicine pentacle teaches us that all lessons are equal, as are all talents and abilities. Native Americans believe that every living creature will one day see and experience each spoke of a medicine wheel and know all those truths. The medicine pentacle is a pathway to truth and peace and harmony and the circle is never ending. The medicine pentacle is life, afterlife, rebirth and the honouring of each step along the way.

The following meditation will help you find your nine spirit guide animals. However, if you already work with one or two main guides you can add them in at the left side and right side positions, if your main animal spirit guide is female, put them on the left, if they are male, put them on the right.

Meditation to Find Your Nine Medicine Pentacle Spirit Guide Animals

Make yourself comfortable and focus on your breathing, deep

breaths in and deep breaths out...

You find yourself on a large flat dusty plain, the sun is warm and you can feel it on your face and body. There are mountain ranges to one side of you and a stream to the other.

You notice a camp fire burning a short distance away from you so you head towards it, when you get closer to the fire you notice a circle of stones placed all around it. You walk slowly around the circle of stones, the point at which you stand has a larger pile of stones and as you walk further you notice another point has a pile of feathers...a bit further round there is a pile of shells, then a terra-cotta bowl with what looks like hot coals in glowing bright red and sending out sparks. Then you notice a smaller circle inside the larger one...this one has just been drawn in the sand and marked at several points, one has a rough star shape, and there is a circle, a heart, a stick man and a stick woman drawing as well.

You pause and look out to the landscape...and then up to the sky...then back to the circles and the fire.

You head towards the pile of feathers and sit on the ground...looking outwards to the east at the landscape with your back towards the fire...allow your eyes to unfocus and your head to clear...an animal comes into you vision, it might be from the sky it might be from the earth, it might be from the mountains or the stream...you ask if it is your east animal guide...and then thank it for being with you.

You move to the next marker, the bowl of hot rocks and sit on the ground, looking outwards to the south at the landscape with your back towards the fire, allow your eyes to unfocus and your head to clear...an animal comes into your vision, it might be from the sky, it might be from the earth, it might be from the mountains or the stream...you ask if it is your south animal guide...and then thank it for being with you.

You move to the next marker, the pile of shells and sit on the ground, looking outwards to the west at the landscape with your back towards the fire, allow your eyes to unfocus and your head to clear...an animal comes into your vision, it might be from the sky, it might be from the earth, it might be from the mountains or the stream...you ask if it is your west animal guide...and then thank it for being with you.

You move to the next marker, the large pile of rocks and sit on the ground, looking outwards to the north at the landscape with your back towards the fire, allow your eyes to unfocus and your head to clear...an animal comes into your vision, it might be from the sky, it might be from the earth, it might be from the mountains or the stream...you ask if it is your north animal guide...and then thank it for being with you.

Then you turn and face the fire, stand up with your arms outstretched and face the sky, allow your eyes to unfocus and your head to clear...an animal comes into your vision ...you ask if it is your above animal guide...and then thank it for being with you.

Then sit on the earth facing the fire and drop your eyes to the ground, allow them to unfocus and your head to clear...an animal comes into your vision... you ask if it is your below animal guide...and then thank it for being with you.

Stay seated, but focus on the flames of the fire, allow your eyes to unfocus and your head to clear...an animal will appear in the flames...you ask if it is your within animal guide and then thank it for being with you.

Now look towards the right of the flames in the fire, allow your eyes to unfocus and your head to clear...an animal will appear in your vision...ask if it is your right side animal guide and then thank it for being with you.

Now look towards the left of the flames in the fire, allow your eyes to unfocus and your head to clear...an animal will appear in your vision...ask if it is your left side animal guide and then thank it for being with you.

Sit for a moment and run through the nine animals that have appeared to you...and then take the bowl of hot stones and add them *to the fire, next take the feathers and throw them up to the winds. Pick up the shells and return them to the stream that runs just a way off from the fire...then walk back to the large pile of stones and send your thanks.*

When you are ready slowly come back to the room...

Write down the animals that you met and what position on the pentacle they were situated. Take some time and research each one then see if their characteristics and energies relate to you. These animals can provide you with a huge amount of support and guidance, come back to meet with them often especially when you need particular guidance.

Shadow Animals

Do you have a fear about a particular animal? There are a few that seem to be favourites for that category, such as spiders and snakes. There is a reason we fear them...they bring us challenges. You might absolutely hate them and not be able to go near one or even watch it on TV or see a photograph of it. My husband has a fear of snakes and has to turn away if an image of one appears on the TV screen. I know people who can't go into a room if they know a spider is in there. The animal may often appear in your nightmares too. These are shadow animals and they bring the life lessons that we are avoiding, the ones that we really do need to learn, but don't want to. It reflects our shadow selves, the part of our personalities that we don't necessarily like very much or the characteristics we wish we didn't have.

It helps to narrow down the fear; do you hate all spiders for instance or is it just the big ones? Or the ones that you think are poisonous and will bite you? Do you hate all snakes or just the ones that can squeeze you to death? With your shadow animal you can work with the same template that we used for your animal spirit guide, writing down all the details about it, where it lives, what it eats etc, but add in a couple of other questions to the list such as, 'Can it physically hurt me?' and, 'What about it do I really hate?'

How do we work with our shadow animal guide? You know what I am going to say don't you? Confront them. Yep sorry, that's about the be all and end all of it. Shadow work is hard, it can take a long time and it is pretty much ongoing, but if you manage to make even a small crack in it then it is so worthwhile.

I am not suggesting you literally confront your shadow animal face on, but you can work with it through meditation, which is hopefully a little less scary. If you have an animal spirit guide that brings you strength, you could meditate and bring your supportive guide with you to meet the shadow one. It is about identifying the feelings, instincts or personality traits that we deny or ignore and bringing them out into the light. Shadow energy is powerful and if you can face it and tap into it then it can be brought to walk beside you rather than fighting against you. Be open and honest with your shadow guide and it will help you understand your own self on a whole different level, it can literally be life-changing.

Animal Spell Working

The magical power in each and every animal – living, extinct or mythical – can be used to assist you in your daily life and can be utilised in spells to aid you in certain situations.

It is nearly impossible to read old collections of magic without seeing something using the energy from animals. I don't mean divination from entrails though…

Throughout history we can see illustrations of animals being used rather than the actual live creature, for instance the Egyptians carried small carvings of cats with them as protection and a 13th century Hebrew text suggests that carving a falcon onto a piece of topaz would ensure the goodwill of leaders, putting a lion on a garnet would bring honour and protection and a bat onto a bloodstone would bring increased power to magical chants.

Get creative, if you want to use the power of an animal for a spell – look around and see what you come up with. Try small figurines, metal charms, pictures from magazines or the internet, product labels, badges, picture playing cards, carvings – the list is endless.

Think about the intent that you want to work your spell for and then ask yourself what animal you associate with that intent. If your spell is for confidence, you might like to draw on the magical powers of peacock or if you need the ability to overcome obstacles then bat or elephant would be an ideal animal to work with.

Here are some references for animals to use for particular intents:

- Call upon the hoarding instincts of the squirrel to help you with your finances.
- Ask the dove to bring you love.

- Invite the courage and cunning of the wolf to help you through a difficult time.
- Invoke a dragon of protection.
- Butterfly emerging from a cocoon brings transformation.
- Fly a winged horse on an astral journey.
- Attune with the masculine spirit of the forest through the mighty stag.
- Seek healing from the dolphin.
- Find the courage of the lion for an interview or a situation that requires it.
- Swan will bring grace.
- Frog or toad bring new beginnings (it's a tadpole thing…).
- Rat can help you overcome hatred.
- Whale can bring balance and relaxation.
- Horse can help you to overcome obstacles (think about it jumping over fences).

Animal Divination, Omens and Superstitions

Animals feature heavily in many divination methods, typically by their symbolic value at the time of observation or by patterns created during ritual sacrifice. While I would not personally advocate ritual animal sacrifice in any way, shape or form, you can observe the wildlife around you, chance encounters and dreams. Although if you do manage to get your hands on small animal bones via road kill or if the animal has been used for food, they do make excellent divination tools.

Get to know your area and read up on animal folklore. There are an incredible amount of sayings that we still use today that actually hold up in fact. The saying that when swallows fly low rain will soon follow has real meaning because swallows like to follow the insects that they feed on and the insects move away from stormy areas. As a method of divination, seeing the swallows flying low means that you need to take an umbrella with you when you go out, but it could also be interpreted that there is a bit of a personal stormy issue heading your way.

Astragalomancy, Scapulimancy, Plastromancy and the Rest

Very long and totally unpronounceable words, but they actually mean divination by animal bones and shells and animal sightings or behaviour.

Astragalomancy is the form of divination using dice marked with letters or numbers, traditionally the dice would have been made from knucklebones or other small bones.

Scapulimancy uses scapulae, which is the proper name for shoulder bones. There were two versions of this form of divination. In one the scapula of an animal was examined after its slaughter and in the second the bone was heated or burnt and then the results were interpreted. The bones would be cleaned after feasting and then held up to the light. Any shadowy or dark patches showing on the bone would be used to foretell the future.

Plastromancy is similar to scapulimancy, but uses turtle plastron. Questions would be put forward and carved onto the shell in oracle bone script, then heat would be applied with a metal rod until the shell cracked. The cracks would be interpreted as answers to the questions.

Osteomancy is the collective name for divination by examination of bones.

In the Yoruba tradition merininlogun is performed, which is divination using a set of 16 cowrie shells. Variations on cowrie shell divination can also be found in Santeria and Candomble practices.

Celts had similar procedures using hot coals and the shoulder bone of a pig, as did Romans using sheep bones. The Greeks cast lots using knucklebones from sheep, while both Zulu tribes and Bantu used a variety of animal bones for various types of divinatory castings.

South African shamans use bones and shells, along with various other natural items for their divinations; this type of divination is also used in Hoodoo. The shaman would use abalone shells for financial questions, cowrie shells in decision-making and spiral shells to determine the best timing for any event in combination with chicken bones, which have different meanings depending on how they land in a casting.

Alectryomancy is rooster divination; the diviner scatters grain on the ground and then observes how a bird – usually a white rooster or cockerel – pecks at it, interpreting the pattern left once the bird has eaten.

A form of apantomancy is divination by chance meeting of animals, such as a black cat crossing your path. Sheesh, black cats get a really bad deal...

Arachnomancy is divination by spiders.

Ancient Romans would interpret the flight of birds. This is called augury, although the word augury can also mean signs that can be interpreted as omens in general. The word ornithomancy is from ancient Greece and means reading omens from the actions of birds, particularly when they take flight or cry.

Batraquomancy is divination with frogs.

Canomancy is prophecy from observing dogs.

Choriomancy is the ability to divine using a pig's bladder.

Conchomancy is divination using a set of shells.

Entomomancy uses insects for predictions.

In Ancient Rome haruspicy was performed; this is the inspection of the entrails of an animal for the purpose of divination and a variation is extispicy which used sacrificed animals, while heptoscopy means reading omens from livers.

Hyomancy is wild hog divination.

Spatilomancy is divination using animal excrement...let's not try that one at home.

Theriomancy covers animal behaviour divination.

Chance Meetings and Sightings

We have probably all been wandering aimlessly down a pathway or across a park when a rabbit or a squirrel jumps in front of us or a crow lands on the fence beside us. We may think nothing of it, but our ancestors would definitely have paid proper attention. Each encounter would have had a very specific meaning.

Here are some examples of bird omens:

Crow cawing from the southeast: Beware of an enemy and bring in some protection.

Dove: Peace and happiness.

Eagle: Success through positive application of personal abilities, so be tenacious.

Magpie: Seeing one magpie is thought to be a very bad omen,

but seeing two is lucky…maybe you could look twice?
Sparrow: Peace in your home, unless it nests on your window then it could mean a bit of love trouble, communicate with each other!

Then we have the rest of the animal kingdom, here are some general omens:

Ant: An ant nest near your home, while annoying, apparently signifies care and guidance from the divine.
Bats: Don't kill a bat…it shortens your own life span (not as much as the bat's though…).
Bees: If they fly around you then it is a sign of messages coming, perhaps from spirit. Landing but not stinging is a sign of good luck (not just because it didn't sting you).
Butterfly: One coming into your home means a wedding or partnership.
Cat: Could be good or bad depending on whether you were doing something decent or not just before you saw it. To kill a cat is a total disaster.
Hare: One seen first thing in the morning is a sign of bad luck, be careful.
Horse: Meeting a horse on your jaunts out means very good news is coming your way.
Moth: One flying toward you brings an important letter or phone call on its wings (not literally obviously).
Mouse: A brown or white one brings good luck, but a grey one brings bad.
Snake: One entering your home brings good luck with it (no thanks…), but if you own a snake and it packs up its bags and leaves then it is a sign of bad luck.

There are some really silly animal omens, but a lot of them are based on some kind of fact or at least loosely so.

Your own pets can also be tools of divination, especially cats:

Washing its face: Visitors are coming; obviously it wants to look its best.

Walking on your cat's tail: Bad luck will follow, not just for the cat.

Stray entering your home: A very good omen that money is on its way to you.

Sneezing: This is good luck for everyone in the home.

Because most people are obsessed with the weather, how about using animals to forecast:

Ants: Stepping on them brings rain (and it is mean).

Chickens: Staying out in the rain means that you should expect rain all day.

Crickets: Chirping loudly means it will be a nice day.

Cows: Restless cows with tails in the air or lying down means rain.

Spider: Spinning in the rain means the rain will stop shortly.

Animals in your Dreams

Dream interpretation dates back for thousands of years, documents from 1350BC in Babylon detail dream symbols. They would look at the entire dream story to ascertain the meaning. Assyrians, however, would look at each individual element in a dream. Egyptians had dream oracles and Hittites prayed to the gods to reveal themselves in their dreams. Native Americans look at dreams as visions that speak to the spirit world.

Here are some animal meanings from your dreams:

Bear: Grumpiness, forbearance, protection, fearlessness.

Bird in a cage: Loss of freedom or the illusion of freedom.

Cat: Recuperative force, new beginnings, mystical energies, an alternative lunar emblem.

Dog: A friendly dog symbolises friendship, but an angry one means arguments.

Dragon: Financial success boost.

Dragonfly: Balance between thought and feeling, potential restlessness, good luck.

Killing an animal: Purposeful banishing of something specific in your life. Consider what that animal represents.

Monkey: Slacking in your personal and spiritual development, unwise action, too much messing about.

Whale: The beginning of a new, but difficult course of action that will come out positively, renewal.

Remember, dream interpretation is highly subjective.

Animal Parts in Magic

It is totally your call as to whether you are comfortable using animal parts in magic, whether it is in spell workings, divination or on your altar to honour the animal. I have a magpie wing, skull and feet on my animal spirit altar, but they came from a road kill bird (that was properly dried out and treated so that the parts don't rot). I also have a set of boar's teeth. I didn't go out and bash the poor animal over the head just to get a pretty decoration for my altar. However, with something like road kill I think it honours the animal to remove it from the road and clean it up. It now sits in pride of place and not only brings the energy of the magpie to my magic, but also serves as a reminder of the cycle of life and death.

If you choose to eat meat then I also think it is only fair to honour the animal. Whenever funds allow, try to purchase organic or farm assured meat (or eggs) and if you are using something like a whole chicken then perhaps think about using the bones once the flesh has been eaten. Chicken bones clean up very well and can be made into a divination set or carved with symbols to make a fetish or even chopped up or ground to go into medicine bags. If you eat the meat then honour the animal by using as much of it as you possibly can without waste.

Bird wings make exceptionally good wafters for sending the smoke around when you are smudging either at home or when in a group circle. Single feathers also work well for the same purpose.

Claws, small bones and antlers can also be used as altar decorations or pieces of jewellery to bring the connection from the animal to you or your circle.

Some items are naturally shed by the animal such as antlers, feathers and snake skins, all of these can be utilised for magical purpose.

Animal parts have been used in magic for thousands of years and some of the items used and their magical properties were recorded. Here is a list of some interesting ones:

Adder: Hang the skin by the chimney to bring good luck or put in the rafters of your house for protection against fire.

Alligator: The tradition of wearing an alligator tooth on a chain as a necklace is said to bring luck and safety.

Ants: Eat their eggs with honey to work as an antidote to love...you would probably have to be quite desperate to try this one...

Bats: These were hung near pigeon houses in ancient Egypt to keep the birds from flying away. In Europe bats were buried at a crossroads with magical herbs as love spells.

Bear: When a member of the family died, a bear head was buried with their body to keep them safe in the afterlife. Romans wore images of the bear or bear claws to ease childbirth and protect the unborn.

Bees: Images of the bee can be found all over the world on ancient sites, especially burial tombs as they were believed to protect the dead and help the soul travel safely to the other world.

Cat: If you find a cat whisker (don't pull it out from the cat...ouch) you can use the whisker in a wishing spell.

Cockerels: The claws bring protection and the blood is used in spells and charms for Voodoo and Santeria practices.

Crow: The bird poop from a crow was used by Aryans in fertility spells...ahem. Native Americans would give a black feather from a crow as a death curse.

Fish: These were eaten by Teutons to absorb their divine properties.

Frog: Frog symbols and ornaments were carried by Egyptians to bring good health and placed in tombs to represent rebirth. Frogs were placed into the mouth of a sick person then sent away to 'take the sickness with it'.

Hare/rabbit: We all know the tradition for carrying a rabbit's foot to bring good luck.

Lion: In ancient Egypt, lion images were placed at the entrance to temples to bring protection and fertility.

Salmon: Eating the flesh of the salmon will bring wisdom and knowledge.

Seal: Romans wore sealskins to bring protection from thunderstorms, which is actually a sensible idea.

Tortoise: Whispering your wish to a tortoise will in turn convey the message direct to a sea god who will then grant it...presumably the message travels to the gods a lot faster than a tortoise walks...

Note: Do check the laws for your area as some places do not allow collection of certain bird feathers.

◊

Animal Magic in Ritual

I have worked a few rituals where we used animal magic to call in the quarters. Each and every animal is associated with one or sometimes two of the elements – earth, air, fire, water – and you can utilise these connections in ritual.

The quarter calls might go something like this:

Spirits of the east, spirits of the air
Spirit of the mighty black raven
Bring to us purification and clarity
Your thought, memory and all seeing
Raven welcome and blessed be!

Spirits of the south, spirits of the flame
Spirit of the warrior wild boar
Bring to us your creativity and passion
Your glow, light and force
Wild boar welcome and blessed be!

Spirits of the west, spirits of the water
Spirit of the beautiful dolphin
Bring to us your deepest intuition and truest emotions
Your strength, power and world walking
Dolphin welcome and blessed be!

Guardians of the north, spirits of the earth
Spirit of the strong wolf
Bring to us your spirit of prosperity
Your leadership, vision and companionship
Wolf welcome and blessed be!

Those animals are just examples – you can work with whatever you feel drawn to, here are some ideas:

Earth animals: Bear, wolf, deer, snake, rabbit, cow, most four legged animals
Air animals: Butterfly, bat, dragonfly, most flying insects, most birds
Fire animals: Lizards, salamanders, phoenix, scorpion, desert creatures, wild cats (lions, tigers etc)
Water animals: Dolphin, whale, seal, crab, seagull, duck, beaver, otter, all fish

Zodiac Animals

You could work with animals from the zodiac that are appropriate for your sun sign because they should be 'in tune' with your personality. I say 'should be' because we know these things aren't always exact and with your zodiac signs it all depends on where the other planets were when you were born too.

Aries: The ram
Taurus: The bull
Gemini: No specific animal, but it is an air sign so most birds would be suitable
Cancer: The crab
Leo: The lion
Virgo: No specific animal, but it is an earth sign so forest dwelling creatures would be suitable
Libra: No specific animal, but it is an air sign so most birds would be suitable
Scorpio: The scorpion
Sagittarius: The centaur, deer/stag or horse
Capricorn: The goat
Pisces: Fish

In Chinese astrology, the year in which you were born is

associated with a particular animal.

Rat: 2008, 1996, 1984, 1972, 1960, 1948, 1936
Ox: 2009, 1997, 1985, 1973, 1961, 1949, 1937
Tiger: 2010, 1998, 1986, 1974, 1962, 1950, 1938
Rabbit: 2011, 1999, 1987, 1975, 1963, 1951,1939
Dragon: 2012, 2000, 1988, 1976, 1964, 1952, 1940
Snake: 2013, 2001, 1989, 1977, 1965, 1953, 1941
Horse: 2014, 2002, 1990, 1978, 1966, 1954, 1942
Goat/ram: 2015, 2003, 1991, 1979, 1967, 1955, 1943
Monkey: 2016, 2004, 1992, 1980, 1968, 1956, 1944
Rooster: 2017, 2005, 1993, 1981, 1969, 1957, 1945
Dog: 2018, 2006, 1994, 1982, 1970, 1958, 1946
Pig: 2019, 2007, 1995, 1983, 1971, 1959, 1947

Celtic Animal Zodiac

This one is a modern invention as far as I can tell although the ancient clans would have been very much connected to the animal world. You can find several variations of this zodiac across the internet.

Dec 24-Jan 20: Stag/deer
Jan 21-Feb 17: Cat or dragon
Feb 18-Mar 17: Adder/snake or seahorse
Mar 18-Apr 14: Fox or hawk
Apr 15-May 12: Cow/bull or sea serpent
May 13-June 9: Seahorse or fox
June 10-July 7: Wren or white horse
July 8-Aug 4: Horse or unicorn
Aug 5-Sep 1: Fish/salmon
Sep 2-Sep 29: Swan
Sep 30-Oct 27: Butterfly
Oct 28-Nov 24: Wolf or hound
Nov 25-Dec 23: Falcon/hawk or horse

There are plenty of resources to look into for more details on both zodiac and Chinese astrology animals if you are interested.

Animal Deities

There are numerous gods and goddesses across the globe that are referred to as 'animal deities' or have particular animals that are sacred to them.

If you work with the gods then you may find that the animal spirit guide that comes to you is also associated with one of the deities you often work with. Or it might be worth investigating to see what deity your animal spirit guide is connected with, you might be pleasantly surprised – synchronicity usually works in mysterious ways!

You can also find out more about your animal spirit guide by researching the gods they are associated with. Below I have listed just a few of the animals and the associated deities. It is by no means comprehensive, but may give you a place to start.

Bears: Artemis (Greek), Artio (Gaulish)
Cats: Bast (Egyptian), Freya (Norse), Hecate (Greek), Cerridwen (Welsh)
Crows: Amaterasu (Japan), The Morrigan/Badb/Macha (Irish), Apollo (Greek)
Cows: Amun (Egypt), Dyaus (India), Hathor (Egypt)
Deer/stag: Finn (Irish), Horned God/Cernnunos, Elen of the Ways (British)
Dogs: Diana (Roman), Papa Legba (West African), Hecate (Greek), Anubis (Egypt)
Dolphins: Anubis (Egypt), Aphrodite (Greek), Poseidon (Greek)
Eagles: Athena (Greek), Ganymede (Greek), Eagle Mother (Native American), Horus (Egypt)
Fox: Loki (Norse), Inari (Japan)
Goats: Aphrodite (Greek), Amalthea (Greek), Baphomet
Horses: Apollo (Roman), Epona (Celtic), Candra (India), Odin

(Norse)

Lion: Isis (Egypt), Sekhmet (Egypt), Ishtar (Babylonian)

Magpies: Apollo (Roman), Skadi (Norse), Hel (Norse)

Owls: Athena (Greek), Blodeuwedd (Welsh), Isis (Egypt)

Peacock: Athena (Greek), Ganymede (Greek), Hera (Greek), Saraswati (Hindu)

Pigs/boars: The Cailleach (Celtic), Varahi (Hindu), Marici (Buddhist), Arduinna (Celtic), Durga (Hindu)

Raven: Odin (Norse), Lugh (Celtic), Bran (Welsh), Morgan le Fay (Celtic)

Snakes: Isis (Egypt), Papa Legba (Haiti), Ra (Egypt), Wadjet (Egypt), Aida Wedo (Haiti)

Spiders: Arachne (Greek), Anansi (African), Spider Woman (Native American), Uttu (Sumerian)

Swans: Aphrodite (Greek), Venus (Roman), Zeus (Greek), Apollo (Greek), Brighid (Celtic), Saraswati (Hindu)

Wolf: The Cailleach (Celtic), Apollo (Greek), Odin (Norse), Cerridwen (Celtic), Cernnunos, Merlin

Wild animals: Aja (Yoruban), Artemis (Greek), Aranyani (Hindu), Herne (Germanic), Diana (Roman)

Animal Magic from Air, Water and Earth

Bird Magic

Many animal spirit guides will come in the form of winged creatures and these have carried magic with them for thousands of years. Many deities have bird sidekicks and all manner of winged fanciful creatures – legends and myths are full of them.

I would imagine to our ancestors a creature that could take to the air would have been quite mystical and so they started to appear in folklore and omens. Birds could foretell death or bring good luck; they were messengers from the gods, angels or souls of the dead.

Not only do they bring the element of air, but also the ability to make a connection between the earth and the sky.

With bird animal guides you not only get the opportunity to work with the animal itself, but also in the form of eggs and feathers, both very magical items. The egg is a complete set of the four elements all in one handy container – the shell represents earth, the inner membrane represents air, the yolk is fire and the white is water. The egg also symbolises the earth, life and renewal.

Feathers are *the* element of air, there couldn't be a more symbolic representation of air unless you could capture a gale in a jar. If you are gifted with a feather make a connection with it, it could be a message for you, it might be from spirit, some think it is a sign of angels or it might be a reminder that you need to make a conscious effort to get out into nature and some believe that a gift of a feather is also a link to the world of Faerie.

If you find a feather give it some thought…what were you thinking about just before you found it? What is going on in your life at the moment? What was your initial thought when you saw it or what words popped into your head? Any of these questions may help determine the reason or it might just be a gift for you to keep for later use.

Feathers have long been associated with omens and the colours have meaning. Here are some traditional colour correspondences, but if you find a coloured feather and it means something else to you…go with your intuition:

Black: Can mean bad luck and was often thought to mean death, but I also think it can be a warning to bring in protection.

Brown: Home, hearth, grounding or friendship.

Grey: Peace.

Black and white: Averting trouble or change is coming.

White: Often said to be a sign the angels are watching over you and faith and hope.

Yellow: Success or acknowledgement that you are on the right path.

Pink: Love.

Blue: A spiritual connection or awakening and inspiration.

Red: Good fortune, passion.

Green: Health, healing or prosperity.

Feathers from particular birds have their own specific meanings too:

Blue Jay feathers: Bring joy, happiness and light.

Crow feathers: Excellent for wisdom, knowledge and helping us to let go of unwanted feelings, thoughts or negative energy.

Robin feathers: Bring new projects, plans and beginnings.

Swan feathers: White swan feathers hold purification, cleansing, beauty and positive energy; black swan feathers can be used to dispel negative energy.

Hawk feathers: Bring the magic of the hunt.

Eagle feathers: Hold huge amounts of energy, but also bring peace, happiness and protection.

Magpie feathers: Bring magic, divination skills, wisdom and change.

Pigeon feathers: Bring peace, love and communication.

Blackbird feathers: Bring poetry, inspiration, music and a stronger connection with meditation.

Use feathers as charms, amulets, talismans, in medicine pouches and in spells. They are a readymade fetish (a charm with magical powers) and can be fashioned into smudge fans, healing sticks, fetish pots, prayer sticks and wands.

World of Insects

This is a huge group of animals, but many of them share the same characteristics as each other and if you meet an insect spirit guide it is worth looking at the group as a whole. It is a very primitive group of beings and can sometimes require a different approach to most animal guides. Insects adapt to their environment, they are industrious and take opportunities that come their way, they are efficient and they metamorphosis.

Under the Sea

The oceans and also rivers and lakes have a diverse and fascinating collection of creatures. If a watery mammal or sea/fresh water fish comes your way then take a very special look at its habitat. Is it fresh water or salt water? Does it have to come up to the surface for air or does it live on the sea bed? Is it a solitary creature or does it swim around in shoals? Does it survive in the cold oceans or thrive in tropical waters? All these things can help you to learn about and understand your animal guide. Being so closely associated with water it will also have the magical properties of healing, cleansing, purification and dealing with emotions.

Reptiles

These creatures are some of the most ancient on this planet and they have survived whatever has been thrown at them, including some of them having survived since the time of the dinosaurs. The main difference with this group of animals is that they are cold blooded and they tend to 'keep their cool' as animal guides and this reflects onto the person. Definitely check out the habitats and way of life for these critters if one has made you its friend.

Animal Meanings

I have included some of the more popular animals here along with mythical ones as well, but it is by no means comprehensive. If an animal comes to you, do as much research as you can. The meanings given here are general with some of my own thoughts and feelings thrown in for good measure. They are not definitive and you may well find different meanings when you start to work with your animal spirit guides.

Ant

Think about a nest full of ants...industrious just doesn't cover it – these little guys work their butts off. They are also part of a community and work together as a team, each one knowing exactly what it needs to do. They also have enormous amounts of patience and determination. They bring honour and respect with them and work together for the good of their community. They also create and design, sometimes huge constructs.

Keywords: Hard work, teamwork, patience, determination, creating your dreams, community and equality.

Badger

A creature of the night and also the wildness of the woods, they are ancient and respected creatures. They are playful and mischievous, but they also work hard creating underground tunnels, which they like to redesign, providing a home for future generations. They can be aggressive, but only when they feel in danger and they will stand their ground and fight for what they want. They are also healers, tapping into the magic of earth to bring relief. Although their sight isn't great they do have an excellent sense of smell and hearing. The badger doesn't mess around, it just gets on with it and gets the job done efficiently. Badger is also very self reliant although with a tendency to hide away from others and is apparently quite house proud.

Keywords: Wisdom, cunning, perseverance, earth magic, protection, creativity, fighting for your rights, organisation, fearless and solitary.

Bat

Some folklore stories suggest that bats were thought to be witches and if one flew close by you it was a witch checking up on you or sending a curse. I think the bat gets a bit of bad press and the horror film industry has not helped. They are in fact beautiful, highly sensitive creatures who bring intuition, dreams and visions. They also have really cool night senses, including night vision and echolocation, which can help you to see through illusions and find the truth. The bat is very sociable and loves nothing more than a good ole chat with the rest of the group. Living in the dark caves of Mother Earth, the bat brings rebirth as it emerges from the depths every night. Bat does, however, require a lot of commitment from you so be warned, it doesn't work with slackers!

Keywords: Commitment, challenges, renewal, rebirth, communication, intuition, sensitivity, illusion, truth and dreams.

Bear

Bear plays a big part in a lot of cultures including Native American and the Celtic tradition, bringing power and protection with it. Don't ever mess with a mama bear who is looking after her babies. Bear hibernates in the winter so may bring a quieter energy during those months, but in spring she brings the magic of new opportunities and possibilities. Her hibernating cycle allows us to do a lot of inner work and self reflection, but it also gives us the ability to know when the time is right and what direction we need to head off in. She brings not only the energy of the sun, but also the moon along with heap loads of intuition too. Bear can be quick to react and has a bit of a temper and a tendency to be a grumpy ole bear at times.

Keywords: Interactions, inner knowledge, introspection, intuition, dreamtime, renewal, moon and sun magic, opportunities, fearlessness and protection.

Beaver

Working like a beaver; he builds, he creates, he achieves everything he sets out to do; he understands how to work as a team, he is persistent and uses whatever he has to hand, and he is a total dam-building genius. Beaver can teach us how to do all of these things and more, appreciating the talents of every individual and working together in harmony. He has grand ideas, but probably not very grand materials, so he works it all out and does the very best job that he can. The houses that beaver builds are strong and secure, built with very good foundations, something we could all do with in our lives...the strong foundations not beaver houses that is...

Keywords: Creativity, building, teamwork, persistence, appreciation, harmony, doing the best we can, strength, security and good foundations.

Bee

Without these little critters whizzing about in their stripy pyjamas we would have no food...they are incredibly important. They are a representation of birth, death and rebirth and have been worshipped and honoured in many cultures for thousands of years. Often mentioned in myths and folklore is the belief that bees are the souls of those that were worthy to come back to earth.

Bees should also be told all the local gossip especially regarding births, deaths and wedding plans...they need to know this stuff. Bees remind us to take the good stuff from life and to literally make hay (or honey) while the sun shines. Bee tells us to follow our dreams, but also with a reminder to plan and save for the future too.

Keywords: Prosperity, good fortune, communication, gossip, reincarnation, goals, celebration, community, achieving your dreams, productivity, co-operation and focus.

Beetle

Beetles come in all shapes and sizes (like humans really) and bring transformation, metamorphosis and rebirth of ideas, thoughts, spirituality and complete lives. Beetles work in harmony with their surroundings and can teach us to do the same, throwing in the ability to use our intuition too. Beetles are also persistent and strong.

Keywords: Transformation, rebirth, spirituality, harmony, intuition, strength and persistence.

Blackbird

The blackbird sings a very sweet song and it is for this that it is probably most well known in myths and folklore. The song can expand our consciousness, heal us and take us on spiritual and magical journeys. Blackbird has often been seen as a gatekeeper to the Otherworld and realms of Faerie. The blackbird has also long been associated with the blacksmith and blacksmith gods who carry their own very special type of magic as the masters of all four elements.

Keywords: Song, communication, healing, spirituality, Otherworld, Faerie, elemental magic, meditation and potential.

Boar

Gorgeous noble creature, the boar has been a symbol of warriors for centuries and features in many battle tales and legends. He is full of masculine energy and brings bravery, balance and strength. Boars are fierce when challenged or when they feel the need to protect themselves or their young. Boar asks you to have faith in your own abilities and to stand up and be counted, moving onwards and upwards putting your fears behind you. Its poor eyesight, but excellent sense of smell and hearing, reminds us to look at everything properly, examining all the details and looking beyond the obvious. Boar will help you to transform, to look within and become the person you wish to be.

Keywords: Self reliance, protection, warrior strength, spirituality, fierceness, nobility, strategy, personal power, re-birth, organisation, leadership, masculine energy, truth and transformation.

Butterfly

The butterfly has to be one of the creatures most associated with transformation and change as it emerges from a cocoon, having changed from a caterpillar to a beautiful winged creature. Just watching a butterfly flit about the garden brings joy and a sense of freedom and happiness. Their bizarre multifaceted eyes allow them to see images incredibly clearly and they can pick up on ultraviolet wavelengths of light so they have the magic of psychic abilities pretty much built in. Look at the butterfly and how it transforms, then watch as it makes the most of life by surrounding itself with colour and nature.

Keywords: Transformation, psychic abilities, changes, beauty, nature, learning, renewal, understanding, happiness and inspiration.

Cat

Those with a cat at home will know that they are gods and should be worshipped and pampered in every way shape and form... Cat definitely brings elegance, independence and intuition and I think it has a definite feminine energy. She is also full of mystery, wisdom and understanding (definitely of how to annoy humans), but she also brings healing and balance – and obviously curiosity (which apparently killed the cat). Cat also comes with definite psychic abilities and always spirituality.

Keywords: Independence, healing, curiosity, mystery, psychic abilities, elegance, intuition, mystery, wisdom, understanding and balance.

Centaur

Half horse, half man resulting in a combination of man and beast – hopefully the best parts of each...

Definitely connected to the starry sky above they can help with a link to astrology or astronomy. The most famous centaur is possibly the symbol of Sagittarius with his bow and arrows. The centaur brings music, healing and knowledge of alchemy. He has a quiver full of inspiration for the arts along with the magical properties of honour and valour. Our valiant beastie also brings help in dealing with the balance of emotions and knowing what desires are good or bad for you.

Keywords: Healing, music, inspiration, creativity, honour, emotions and desires.

Chicken

Chicken is all about fertility with a bit of sacrifice thrown in for good measure. The fertility comes from their egg-laying ability and the sacrifice bit from...well...being a sacrificial animal of choice throughout history. She does bring with her the essence of motherhood, nurturing, domestic bliss, being broody and fussing about. Chicken is in tune with the earth and heralds prosperity, rebirth and renewal.

Keywords: Fertility, sacrifice, rebirth, motherhood, nurturing, abundance, comfort, broodiness and fussing.

Cockerel

The cockerel carries a slightly different magic from the chicken... The cockerel is often linked to the Underworld and is a guardian, but is also another one for sacrifice. Cockerel is said to not only predict the weather, but also to use his power of psychic abilities to warn of impending danger. This feathered fowl likes to strut his funky stuff; he is all about sexuality and fertilisation, after all he usually has an entire hen house of chickens to service... With his early rising and crowing about the sun rising he is also linked to renewal and rebirth. The cockerel (or rooster) also appears in the Chinese zodiac and brings humour, eccentricity and enthusiasm.

Keywords: Sexuality, psychic abilities, sacrifice, fertility, renewal, humour, eccentricity and enthusiasm.

Cow/Bull

A whole load of bull...or cow...

Both are very symbolic of fertility although the cow obviously brings mothering instincts into play as well. The bull is very masculine and embodies the solar energy of the sun whereas the cow is feminine personified and signifies the energy of the moon; they make a nice balance. The bull is also the symbol of the zodiac sign Taurus, which is an earth sign and I think both the cow and the bull have earthy connections. These are both all about being productive, starting new projects or feeling stubborn or even insecure.

Keywords: Fertility, motherhood, sun and moon magic, stubbornness, insecurity, productive, earth magic, stability, aggression, defence, contentment and strength.

Crocodile/Alligator

The good ole croc can see incredibly well, which has led to its association with clarity and clear thought. Although it has often been linked to a destructive kind of power, it can show us great knowledge and how the cycle of life, death and rebirth works. They are a primordial force that has connections to the land and the water. Their main role is that of water guardians, defending and keeping the secret mysteries of the deep. Crocodiles shed tears, not real ones, but just to lubricate their eyes (apparently) and this could be a sign that we aren't showing or acknowledging our true emotions.

Keywords: Clarity, truth, visions, cycle of life, rebirth, emotions, mysteries and secrets.

Crow

This is one very powerful animal spirit guide and a clever whatsit as well. Crow brings wisdom, knowledge and magic from every dimension and helps us to learn to trust our own intuition. He is also mindful, not just of our own self, but also in judging others actions and words. Crow is very much an eccentric individual and he encourages that in those he chooses to walk with. Crow also brings change, creation, spiritual strength and the ability to see into the past and the future. He is a bit of a cheeky sly one though and deception is not beneath him. In fact sometimes he revels in it. He does teach us to adapt, to look beyond the ordinary and to listen to what is going on around us.

Keywords: Mindfulness, truth, trust, intuition, integrity, individuality, change, past/present/future, spiritual strength, magic, wisdom, deception and awareness.

Deer/Stag

Beautiful elegant and graceful creatures, both the stag and the deer are royalty within the woods and are sacred in many cultures. A white hart is often depicted as a messenger from the Otherworld that can guide you on your spiritual quest. Stag is a creature of the hunt with strength, courage and power. Both like to graze during dawn and dusk and these are in between times when the veil between our world and the Otherworld is hazy.

Keywords: Grace, reaching your goals, alertness, hunt, intuition, listening, transformation, observation, decisions, Otherworld, spirituality, messages, gentleness, innocence and adventure.

Dog

A dog animal spirit guide is for life, not just for Yule…definitely man (or woman's) best friend and so jam packed with loyalty you couldn't fit in another wet slobbery lick. Dog is devoted, but also a protector, a companion, faithful and hardworking. Dog is also good with communication, especially if he needs a walk…he can also provide healing and support. The 'black dog' is a creature that foretells impending doom and also a term used for depression so this dark side of dog can also be a warning system.

Keywords: Loyalty, devotion, protection, companion, faithful, hard work, communication, healing, support and warning.

Dolphin

It might be a mammal, but it lives in the sea. Dolphins were often thought to be an indication that storms were coming and sailors believed that dolphins charmed the winds. They are incredibly intelligent and also very playful, enjoying life on the ocean waves, but they also bring healing and balance.

Keywords: Wisdom, playfulness, healing, balance, freedom, change, communication, trust, harmony, emotions and water magic.

Donkey

Donkeys are eager and versatile workers that have served human kind for thousands of years. They take on huge burdens and responsibilities generally without complaint although they can be 'stubborn as a mule'. Donkey could indicate that you are always willing to help others, but maybe that you need to make sure you don't take on too much, you also have to look after yourself, you can always say no. If a donkey feels uncomfortable about a situation he won't carry on, not because he is stubborn as suggested, but because his intuition is sending a warning; this is also a reminder to us – trust your intuition and know your limita-tions and boundaries.

Keywords: Versatility, burdens, responsibilities, helping others, look after yourself, intuition, stubbornness and limitations.

Dragon

Phewy this is a huge section and needs an entire book to itself. However, if dragon has come to you then it will probably be a particular colour or type, whether it is an elemental dragon (earth, air, fire, water), a region one (ice, sand, snow etc) or a cultural one (Chinese, Welsh etc) the range is endless. Each one will bring its own very special and unique characteristics and qualities. The basic qualities of a dragon are strength and courage, but they can bring all kinds of messages and magical properties to aid us in life. They are a very primordial energy and incredibly powerful.

Keywords: Strength, courage, energy – other meanings are specific to the type of dragon.

Dragonfly

Flitting in and out of reeds and water plants, the dragonfly is a master of flight who reflects light and colours. This is one magical and mystical creature that is often associated with the world of Faerie. Dragonfly brings illusion, shape-shifting, changes, transformation, emotions and compassion along with wingfuls of healing energy. Dragonfly helps us to see beyond the normal and the reality into other realms to unleash possibility and changes within ourselves and the magic that the world has to offer us.

Keywords: Magic, mystery, illusion, shape-shifting, change, transformation, emotions, compassion, healing, possibilities and enlightenment.

Eagle

The mighty eagle immediately makes you sit up straight and take notice; he is a bird of immense power, courage, majesty and authority. As he flies through the skies he helps us to raise our vibrations and our expectations to see things from a higher view point, he guides us to inspect every aspect of our own world so that we can achieve our goals.

Keywords: Strength, courage, wisdom, knowledge, hidden truths, perspective, spiritual direction and goals.

Elephant

Huge hefty creatures, but oh so gentle, the elephant is a great remover of obstacles and barriers, not just physically, but also emotionally, mentally and spiritually. They love to learn new things and have tremendous amounts of patience. Elephant can help you take on new challenges or teachings and give you the confidence to run with it. Elephant is strong and protective, but also caring, supportive and nurturing.

Keywords: Removing obstacles, strength, wisdom, confidence, patience, learning, commitment, gentleness, compassion and support.

Fox

The wily cunning ole fox has appeared in myths and legends for centuries bringing his shape-shifting and healing abilities with him. He is skilful, creative and full of the mystical dawn/dusk in between magic that is also often associated with the world of Faerie. He can teach us his cunning and clever ways using camouflage, agility and the art of shape-shifting. He doesn't out run...he observes, plans, plots and schemes, anticipating the next move and outwitting those that chase him. He is smart and crafty, but he does go over the top sometimes and becomes unbearably so.

Keywords: Cunning, stealth, courage, observation, persistence, wisdom, magic, shape-shifting and invisibility.

Frog/Toad
It was once believed that toads were witches who had shape-shifted…seriously if I was going to shape-shift it wouldn't be into a toad…but it does mean that toad brings cauldrons full of magic and witchcraft with it. Both creatures have very similar magical properties; the frog is just slightly damper. They are a representation of rebirth and new life and also a symbol of awakening…have you kissed any frogs lately? Patience is definitely one of the virtues frog brings as they spend hours sitting still waiting for their prey. The tadpole into frog scenario also creates the powers of transformation and water brings emotions and intuition.

Keywords: Magic, witchcraft, rebirth, new life, awakening, patience, transformation, emotions and intuition.

Goat
The symbol for the sign of Capricorn and associated with several horned gods; the goat is a feisty ole thing. He climbs ridiculously high sloping mountains with total sure-footedness and likes to butt heads. Basically goat adapts to his surroundings and is an all-round survivor, finding his way through any kind of unexplored territory or terrain.

Keywords: Independence, strength, survival, foundations, security, growth, new pathways, confidence, stubbornness and direction.

Grasshopper
The grasshopper sings with its body parts (but apparently generally only the males) and can leap over huge obstacles or into other dimensions, now that's something not everyone can claim to do. They are also ancient and have a very strong medicine connection to ancestors. Grasshopper brings good luck and abundance, but also offers up opportunities for you to just leap right into, asking you to trust and not always to look before you

leap. Jump forwards...never back.

Keywords: Astral travel, overcoming obstacles, change, ancestors, luck, abundance, opportunity and looking forward.

Griffin

With the head, wings and claws of an eagle at the front and the body and tail of a lion, this animal may come across as being a bit confused. What he actually brings is protection, guardianship and retribution where needed. He is incredibly powerful and full of all things magical. His hearing is excellent and he listens not only to what people are saying out loud, but also the inner thoughts as well. He symbolises the sun and the elements of both earth and air. His pathway is one of spiritual enlightenment.

Keywords: Spiritual wisdom, enlightenment, guidance, guardian, protection, vengeance, power, magic and listening.

Hedgehog

Often associated with the world of Faerie, in fact it is sometimes suggested that the hedgehog is a faery or even a witch in disguise... Linked with witchcraft, the hedgehog has good and bad folklore superstitions. Hedgehogs are mostly active at dawn and dusk, the in-between times, so they have links to the Otherworld, prophecy and psychic abilities. The hedgehog is probably best known for its defence mechanism of rolling into a ball to present its sharp spines to the world, keeping it safe from predators, reflecting the ability to deal with challenges calmly and effectively. Definitely an earth element creature, the hedgehog brings a huge pack of earth magic along with abundance and fertility.

Keywords: Faerie, witchcraft, psychic abilities, prophecy, Otherworld, defence, challenges, calm, earth magic, abundance and fertility.

Hippopotamus

A very powerful animal spirit that is chocked full of deep emotional energy, imagination and ideas. Its name translates as 'water horse' and it does spend most of the day in the water, which brings the emotions, intuition and healing. It is also very physically strong and can help bring grounding energy when we have a bit of an emotional hissy fit. The water connection also brings creativity and inspirational flow. They do tend to keep just a part of their heads above the water so that they know what is going on even when mostly submerged, so they see and hear without losing perspective.

Keywords: Emotions, imagination, intuition, healing, strength, grounding, creativity, inspiration, awareness and perspective.

Horse

The horse seems to have devoted a huge part of its existence to serving mankind (thank you horseys). It works hard, carries, transports and is a companion – even the power of our cars is still measured in 'horse power'. The horse shoe can be seen on many buildings, hung as a symbol of prosperity and good luck. There are several horse symbols carved into hillsides across the UK, all of which are associated with fertility. Horses have also played a very important part in many wars throughout the ages, bringing their power and strength with them. Hobby horses have also appeared in our history linked again with fertility and to ensure abundance of the crops.

Keywords: Friendship, faithfulness, freedom, endurance, power, energy, travel, loyalty, overcoming obstacles, fertility and strength.

Ladybird/Ladybug

Called a ladybird in the UK and ladybug in the USA, this tiny little pretty coloured insect is a powerful animal spirit guide. The shell keeps it protected, the wings allow it to fly and it has amazing instincts, feeling vibrations through its legs to allow it to sense the energy of whatever it is touching. The bright colours also serve as a warning to predators to keep away, guiding us to send out the same message to our enemies. The colours of this little bug also bring happiness and joy and remind us to let go of fears and live life to the fullest. The ladybird asks us to trust and have faith, not just in ourselves, but also in those around us too. Ladybird also brings a connection to our past lives, death and rebirth, renewal and spiritual enlightenment.

Keywords: Trust, faith, wishes, luck, protection, happiness, intuition, defence, past lives, cycle of life and enlightenment.

Lion

This has to be one of the most popular animal guides linked to courage and strength...rawr! Lions live in family groups (prides) and share the hunting duties; essentially they are quite laid back about life in general. Male lions are associated with the solar gods and lionesses with the mother goddesses including maternity and vengeance.

Keywords: Sun magic, goddess magic, hunting, community, sharing, protection, strength, courage, co-operation, maternity, vengeance, being heard, relaxation, family and stress release.

Lizard

Lizards like the best of both worlds in that they love to bask in the sun, but also to swim in the water and they have their own in-built heat regulator as they are cold blooded. If their tail should happen to be lost (careless) it will re-grow. In ancient myths they symbolise wisdom and good fortune, but also death and rebirth.

Keywords: Facing your fears, guidance, balance, re-birth, wisdom, good fortune and the cycle of life.

Magpie

This black-and-white mystical bird brings feathers full of occult knowledge. The magpie is also known as a Jack of all trades, but master of none – dabbling in everything. It is a reminder that whatever task you take on, do it properly and follow it through to completion. Magpie has the ability to open a gateway to the world of spirit and the Faerie realms; he can also help with past life exploration. Be warned though…messing with magic can have consequences and magpie medicine has a tendency to be unpredictable. Magpie is also very vocal (they sit in my garden and shout if there is no food about…). Magpie also loves shiny things, which is a warning not to fall prey to the lure of too many material things in life.

Keywords: Occult, magic, knowledge, dedication, spirit world, Faerie, past life, consequences, communication, clarity, opportunistic, perception, illusion and expression.

Mole

A big part of mole medicine is the ability to trust your senses and your instincts and to be able to 'feel' the truth or a lie. Mole lives under the ground so makes an excellent guide to the Underworld and to mysteries and secrets. Mole has faith and can guide you on your spiritual journey.

Keywords: Trust, senses, instincts, truth, guidance, Underworld, mysteries, faith and spirituality.

Monkey

Definitely one of the main characteristics of monkey is playing around…but they don't play randomly, they are in fact particularly choosey about who they play with, perhaps a reminder that there is a time and a place for humour. Monkeys display compassion, understanding and a deep sense of bonding, they also like to groom, providing support and love to family members. They have a complex communication system, which can be very vocal. Also take a look at the position a monkey holds within a group and relate it to your own position within your social and work structure. Don't forget...these creatures are not shy!

Keywords: Honour, instinct, community, mobility, protection, playfulness, humour, compassion, understanding and communication.

Mouse

The mouse was apparently one of Apollo's sacred creatures...if it is good enough for Apollo it is good enough for anyone. Mice are um...let's just say they are prolific...so they represent not only fertility, but abundance too. Mice are also home lovers and love to burrow, so they have a strong connection to the Underworld. Mouse does have some dark myths associating it with death, but this may derive from later times and the plague. However, mice do actually keep themselves very clean and well groomed. They are also industrious, ingenious and good hoarders, conserving their resources. Mouse is also known to be very timid and nervous, so may be telling you to look at your behaviour.

Keywords: Fertility, abundance, home, Underworld, death, cleanliness, industrious, ingenious, hoarding, reserves and behaviour.

Octopus

Quite a deep, meaningful and complicated animal spirit guide this one...take your time and really explore all the symbolism that octopus brings to the table. She has all the usual attributes of the water element, but also ties in with moon magic. Her environment is always moving and on the change and she adapts easily to cope with it all. She is a spiritual creature, but one that lives in contact with the ocean bed so she is also very grounded. Octopus has the bizarre ability to detach a limb if she is caught by a predator, which reflects us being able to cut loose all that weighs us down.

Keywords: Emotions, moon magic, adaptability, spirituality, grounding, letting go, mystery and creativity.

Otter

Otter is definitely a water animal, but also with a strong connection to the earth element too. Otters do like to play and certainly remind us to enjoy life and not be too serious. Otter is also extremely curious with a love of exploring, he shows us how to let go of the past and that which no longer serves so that we can move forward with a skip in our step. They have a very powerful feminine energy with strong sisterhood tones. Otter is caring, creative and nurturing and just likes to bob along with the ebb and flow of life.

Keywords: Guidance, psychic abilities, faithfulness, playfulness, exploration, curiosity, recovery, feminine energy, caring, creativity and nurturing.

Owl

There are lots of myths and legends about this beautiful bird of the night and some conflict between good and bad. Owl will defend itself and the nest of its young, but it also has an offbeat approach to parenting where some chicks may starve due to lack of food or be killed off by siblings. It is a creature of the between times, choosing to fly at dawn, dusk and during the dark of the night, so it tends to have connections to gods of death in many cultures. Some say that to hear an owl screech means impending doom… Owl is another creature that was said to be a witch that had shape-shifted.

Keywords: Protection, witchcraft, magic, death and rebirth, silence, swiftness, deception (uncovering), Underworld, wisdom, dreams, shape-shifting, messages, secrets and omens.

Panther/Leopard

This category covers panthers, leopards, jaguars and cougars as they all have the same or very similar characteristics. They are extremely fierce, treacherous, malicious and savage, but they are also intelligent and quick to learn. These animals bring bravery, courage, boldness and a beautiful grace. Panther can teach you how to pace yourself and allow time to rest and play in between getting the job done. However, panther is always the first and fastest to respond to any situation and deals well with deadlines and pressure. Panther can also give guidance within your personal and professional life. Panther is a feminine energy, the dark goddess and the dark of the moon and is a symbol of death and rebirth.

Keywords: Malice, fierceness, bravery, courage, grace, pacing yourself, pressure, timeframes, life, death and rebirth.

Peacock

The male peacock likes to strut his funky stuff and with a beautiful tail full of feathers wouldn't you too? He brings heap loads of self esteem, nobility, vitality and the ability to walk tall and stand proud. Peacock also brings benevolence, patience, kindness, compassion and good luck. In complete opposition to the peacock's beautiful appearance it cannot sing to save its life, instead its shrieks are said to be the sound of the Underworld...guess you can't have everything in life. The feathers bring a mixed message, some say to have the feathers in your home brings unhappiness, but others believe the feather is one of protection against evil and negativity...go with your intuition on this one.

Keywords: Dignity, self esteem, confidence, protection, patience, kindness, compassion, luck, Underworld and nobility.

Phoenix

A beautiful bird from mythology with fiery coloured plumage

that echoes the colours from a glowing fire. The phoenix sacrifices itself by bursting into flame and then rising again reborn from the ashes, which makes it an incredibly strong spirit animal for death and rebirth. Said to only eat air, it lives a very solitary life in the middle of nowhere, appearing among humans only when it is ready to build its nest and die among the flames. The tears of a phoenix are said to have amazing healing powers. Being associated with the element of fire (obviously...) it brings all the correspondences that fire has to offer – passion, strength, creativity and the ability to rise above issues.

Keywords: Death and rebirth, renewal, healing, passion, strength, creativity and growth.

Rabbit/Hare

Rabbits and hares like to make lots of baby rabbits and hares...so fertility is key here. They also have a strong connection to the seasons and the moon. Rabbits like to live in burrows, which also gives them an earthy grounded energy. Hares do not dig burrows, but instead live above ground and are good at finding cover to hide in fields and meadows. Rabbits and hares are both nocturnal, linking them to intuition, emotions and reflection. They are very sociable animals and love a bit of a rabbit get together, but they can also show aggression and jealousy when provoked – much the same as any family or community. They are alert and sensitive to the environment around them and very cautious, but they also like to have a good hop and a skip.

Keywords: Fertility, seasons, moon magic, earth energy, intuition, emotions, reflection, social, community, jealousy, sensitivity, caution and joy.

Rat

Such a misunderstood creature and blamed incorrectly for so many things. Its connection to death started way before the Black Death as it is a sacred animal of the Underworld, carrying spiritual wisdom rather than plague-ridden fleas. In some cultures the rat is also considered to bring fertility and wealth. Rats are definitely cunning and resilient creatures and although they do like to forage in the rubbish bins they are actually very clean animals. Did you know that rats actually share their food with each other too? And they help each other out.

Keywords: Spirituality, wisdom, fertility, wealth, cunning, resilience, cleanliness, sharing, kindness, helpfulness and resourcefulness.

Raven

A very mystical and magical bird, which appears in myths and legends connected with the occult and dark gods and goddesses across the globe. They were often feared because of their habit of feeding on the corpses of the dead hanging from the gallows (ewwww). However, raven was just doing its bit in the natural cycle of life. Raven has the power to help you shift consciousness and enter other realms and dimensions; he is also a shape-shifter himself. Keeper of secrets, magic and transformation, the raven can help you uncover and work with your inner fears. He brings lightness to the dark helping to resolve inner conflicts. Raven will bring changes to your life and put the spark back into your magical and spiritual world.

Keywords: Introspection, courage, magic, healing, rebirth, secrets and shape-shifting.

Robin

Tiny birds...big medicine. A bird of sacrifice and rebirth it also brings happiness, wisdom, change, growth and renewal. The robin is also a very caring and nurturing parent. Robin helps you to let go of the past and come out renewed and refreshed. Robin is very territorial, creative and a guide to trusting your intuition. Let go of any dramas or issues and learn to sing a happy robin song.

Keywords: Happiness, guidance, change, growth, renewal, wisdom, nurturing, creativity and intuition.

Scorpion

Scorpion is a solitary creature who prefers his own company although he does like the occasional passionate, controlling sexual fling. The life of a scorpion is definitely one of intense short-lived passion followed by longer bouts of self imposed (and preferred) solitary. Defence, control and protection are keywords here. A sun-filled creature that has a definite sting in its tail, Scorpion can also be scared of feeling vulnerable. It looks a bit dismal at first, but if scorpion has come to you, have a look at the areas of your life that it might reflect...

Keywords: Transition, sex, control, solitary, passion, protection, defence and vulnerability.

Seagull

The members of the gull species (which are numerous) can survive for long periods of time without food and survive under generally terrible conditions so he brings cunning and perseverance, but he also has a very naughty and mischievous side including being selfish and argumentative. He is a scavenger and will eat pretty much anything...and he is loud, very loud! Some myths tell of them being messengers from the gods so they provide a link to the Otherworld. Although they are found on the seashore and love to bob about on the water they actually live on the land and never venture far from the shore, which makes them 'inbetweenys' and gives them a link to the world of Faerie. The seagull also brings the element of earth and of water and all the associations they carry with them.

Keywords: Emotions, survival, cunning, perseverance, mischievous, selfish, arguments, scavenger, messenger, spirit world, Otherworld, Faerie, communication and behaviour.

Seal

Myths and legends tell of the seal being able to shape-shift into human form, these magical creatures are often referred to as selkies. Seals live most of their life in the water, but they do come ashore to bask in the sun and to give birth. Their deep connection to the sea echoes the rhythms of life and going with the ebb and flow. Water is also creative and full of imagination, inspiration and intuition. Seals are keepers of mysteries and can teach us how to bring balance and harmony to our lives.

Keywords: Transformation, ebb and flow, emotions, imagination, inspiration, intuition, mysteries, balance, harmony, creativity and changes.

Shark

Sharks have perhaps gotten a bit of a bad reputation over the years and although it is fair to say a large group of sharks can be dangerous and unpredictable, they are really quite peaceful creatures. They can, however, be called upon to lend you courage, protection and confidence to 'fend off' any unwanted attention. Obviously they have a very strong connection to the element of water and for anyone finding this animal as a guide it would be worth researching their feeding, living environments and patterns to see how they reflect your own. Shark also brings visions, prophecy and a psychic connection to spirit – and the power to keep busy and active, sometimes too much.

Keywords: Unpredictable, courage, protection, confidence, water magic, visions, psychic work, activity, hunter, survival, adaptability, independence, emotions and balance.

Sheep

It might seem an unlikely animal spirit guide, but it has some interesting medicine to offer...

Sheep are innocent and vulnerable and most definitely connected to the dream world, as in counting them to go to sleep.

It could also mean you are perhaps 'following along like a sheep' and conforming to the will of others a little too much. Sheep will ask you to look at the areas of your life where you feel overwhelmed or vulnerable and maybe even powerless and will help you do something about it. On the flip side, sheep could also help you to get in touch with a softer side of your personality.

Keywords: Innocence, vulnerability, healing, dreams and inner work.

Snail

Okay so it probably wouldn't be your first choice for an animal spirit guide, but if it comes your way don't argue...go with it, there will be a reason. One of the main purposes for snail's arrival is to bring you patience by the slime load. Snail knows that good things come to those who wait and anything important is worth doing properly and at a steady pace; life is all too fast and we should all slow down and give ourselves time to smell the roses. Snails are generally quite small so also bring the message that you might need to focus on the detail and take notice of the smaller things. And, of course, the snail is protected by an outer shell so it brings protective qualities as well as the idea that sometimes you need to withdraw and have some 'me time'.

Keywords: Patience, protection, spiral of life, letting go of deadlines, slowing down, paying attention to details, inner work and withdrawal.

Snake

Quite often a shadow guide, the snake has so many wonderful qualities that will help and guide you. It sheds its skin, which reminds us that we can shed our illusions and any self-imposed limitations or ideas and brings a link to astral travel. Snake also brings fertility, creation and transformation. He is a symbol of sexuality and linked with many deities for that same reason. Snake is energy, raw power and our inner spark of spirituality, but he also brings healing and wisdom.

Keywords: Transformation, fertility, astral travel, creativity, sexuality, power, spirituality and healing, wisdom.

Spider

Another creature that a lot of people are afraid of, but really they are incredibly magical and have a lot to teach us. They weave the web of fate and bring a balance between the past and future bringing spirituality and creativity. Spider brings awareness of your own web of life and how you create and design everything that happens around you. Spider hands back the responsibility of creating your own environment to you, with a reminder that you are in charge.

Keywords: Creation, weaving reality, infinity, balance, past/present/future, responsibility and spirituality.

Squirrel

Squirrel is a puzzle solver, there are not many obstacles that the squirrel can't work his way out of or over and he does so with complete perseverance. He is also a hoarder, packing away food to sustain him over the winter months; this guy is totally prepared, but he only takes what he needs. These things are good guidelines for us to follow. Squirrels also like to have a bit of a party and play around in between doing all the jobs that need doing along with periods of just sitting quietly and watching the world go by. They also like a good chit chat and can be quite trusting.

Keywords: Removing obstacles, solving problems, resource-fulness, preparing, planning ahead, balance, knowing when to rest, playful, action, communication and trust.

Swan

These beautiful graceful creatures bring inner beauty, self esteem and innocence as they glide along the surface of the water. Swan is also associated with love, poetry and music and is often referred to in myths as representing the soul of a person. It is also worth looking at the story of the ugly duckling, the baby bird that others rejected and ridiculed…who grew up to be a beautiful swan. Swan also brings the ability to tap into your intuition and psychic abilities bringing about altered states of awareness. Swan teaches us to go with the flow and accept that which we cannot change. Swans also mate for life and are dedicated to their partners making a commitment that is bonding.

Keywords: Beauty, self-esteem, love, the arts, inspiration, inner self, intuition, psychic abilities, going with the flow, acceptance, dedication, commitment and respect.

Tiger

Tiger is primal, unpredictable, trusts its own intuition and is spontaneous; all qualities that a tiger animal guide brings with him. Tiger is willpower, personal strength and courage and is filled with both negative and positive energy. He can help you to overcome issues or problems and release the inner strength to reach your full potential. Tiger also has physical strength, vitality and the ability to heal. His other sides show aggression and predatory instincts. He asks you to think about your deep feelings and emotions and what those strong emotions are connected to.

Keywords: Emotions, intuition, spontaneity, power, personal strength, courage, overcoming obstacles, vitality, healing and aggression.

Unicorn

A mythical creature (or not…) stories about the unicorn can be found throughout the world. Usually the unicorn is depicted as pure white with a long spiral horn (the allicorn) on its forehead, but it has been described as being many other colours. Unicorn is pure and innocent, which is why children will often connect very well with this animal spirit guide. They are full of magic and enchantment and often linked with the Faerie world. They are said to be so fast that no one can ever catch one if they chase it, but if it comes to you it can bring transformation, prosperity, strength, success, spirituality, changes, and valour.

Keywords: Purity, innocence, magic, enchantment, Faerie, speed, transformation, prosperity, strength, success, spirituality, changes and valour.

Vulture

So it might not be the most attractive of animal spirit guides, but hey who are we to judge? The vulture has long been held in high regard by many cultures and is often a symbol of protection, destruction and compassion. But he does a good service; he is part of the cycle of life and nature's cleanup crew. Vulture appears quite a lot in the Egyptian myths, often as a headdress or his feathers used in rites. Vulture can teach you how to 'read' people and their auras, but also how to get noticed for your work – vulture is all about actions rather than words. He is a very powerful animal to align with and can teach you to utilise your own energy efficiently, but also how to connect with the energy of the earth. His excellent vision will also show you how to see into this world and the next.

Keywords: Protection, destruction, compassion, service, cycle of life, all seeing, action, energy, earth magic, visions and psychic abilities.

Whale

The whale always seems to me to have an immense wisdom, not just the usual knowledge, but also ancient age-old information. He is said to be a record keeper of all eternity with the power of water to go with it. Whale song is hauntingly beautiful and brings the magic of rhythm and sound, teaching us to hear our inner voice. Whale is definitely a spiritual and psychic creature who can help us tap into our own abilities.

Keywords: Wisdom, knowledge, ancestors, rhythms of life, inner voice, spirituality, psychic abilities, creativity, truth and imagination.

Wolf

Wolf spirit animal guide is a teacher, a pathfinder and a guardian who helps us to understand ourselves and others. He brings new ideas and steers us in the right direction to learn new things and gain the knowledge and wisdom that we seek. Wolves are usually found in packs, taking on the responsibilities of family and they are territorial; prepared to protect themselves. Due to their sensitive and intuitive nature, they can also spot deceit or hidden agendas straight away.

Keywords: Teacher, pathways, guardian, understanding, new ideas, knowledge, wisdom, community, responsibilities, protection, sensitivity, intuition and truth.

Wren

This teeny tiny bird brings a huge magical punch of animal medicine in the form of new energy, activity and sparks your mental and emotional vibes. Wren helps you to see into the dark with exacting clarity, helping guide you in your dreams and meditations as well. Wren gives guidance with relationships of all kinds whether it is family, friends or work colleagues. He lightens your heart and shows you the meaning of true happiness along with determination, resourcefulness and strength to achieve your goals. Wren also brings balance of emotions and feelings allowing you to listen to your inner voice.

Keywords: Energy, activity, emotions, dreams, guidance, relationships, happiness, determination, resourcefulness, strength and balance.

Animal Endings

Whatever pathway your animal magic journey takes you on; pay attention, listen and trust your guide – the animal kingdom has much to teach us. Don't take your animal spirit guide for granted, work together for an amazing experience.

Moon Books

PAGANISM & SHAMANISM

What is Paganism? A religion, a spirituality, an alternative belief system, nature worship? You can find support for all these definitions (and many more) in dictionaries, encyclopaedias, and text books of religion, but subscribe to any one and the truth will evade you. Above all Paganism is a creative pursuit, an encounter with reality, an exploration of meaning and an expression of the soul. Druids, Heathens, Wiccans and others, all contribute their insights and literary riches to the Pagan tradition. Moon Books invites you to begin or to deepen your own encounter, right here, right now. If you have enjoyed this book, why not tell other readers by posting a review on your preferred book site. Recent bestsellers from Moon Books are:

Journey to the Dark Goddess
How to Return to Your Soul
Jane Meredith
Discover the powerful secrets of the Dark Goddess and transform your depression, grief and pain into healing and integration.
Paperback: 978-1-84694-677-6 ebook: 978-1-78099-223-5

Shamanic Reiki
Expanded Ways of Working with Universal Life Force Energy
Llyn Roberts, Robert Levy
Shamanism and Reiki are each powerful ways of healing;
together, their power multiplies. *Shamanic Reiki* introduces
techniques to help healers and Reiki practitioners tap ancient
healing wisdom.
Paperback: 978-1-84694-037-8 ebook: 978-1-84694-650-9

Pagan Portals – The Awen Alone
Walking the Path of the Solitary Druid
Joanna van der Hoeven
An introductory guide for the solitary Druid, *The Awen Alone*
will accompany you as you explore, and seek out your own
place within the natural world.
Paperback: 978-1-78279-547-6 ebook: 978-1-78279-546-9

A Kitchen Witch's World of Magical Herbs & Plants
Rachel Patterson
A journey into the magical world of herbs and plants, filled with
magical uses, folklore, history and practical magic. By popular
writer, blogger and kitchen witch, Tansy Firedragon.
Paperback: 978-1-78279-621-3 ebook: 978-1-78279-620-6

Medicine for the Soul
The Complete Book of Shamanic Healing
Ross Heaven
All you will ever need to know about shamanic healing and
how to become your own shaman...
Paperback: 978-1-78099-419-2 ebook: 978-1-78099-420-8

Shaman Pathways – The Druid Shaman
Exploring the Celtic Otherworld
Danu Forest
A practical guide to Celtic shamanism with exercises and
techniques as well as traditional lore for exploring the Celtic
Otherworld.
Paperback: 978-1-78099-615-8 ebook: 978-1-78099-616-5

Traditional Witchcraft for the Woods and Forests
A Witch's Guide to the Woodland with Guided Meditations and
Pathworking
Melusine Draco
A Witch's guide to walking alone in the woods, with guided
meditations and pathworking.
Paperback: 978-1-84694-803-9 ebook: 978-1-84694-804-6

Wild Earth, Wild Soul
A Manual for an Ecstatic Culture
Bill Pfeiffer
Imagine a nature-based culture so alive and so connected,
spreading like wildfire. This book is the first flame…
Paperback: 978-1-78099-187-0 ebook: 978-1-78099-188-7

Naming the Goddess
Trevor Greenfield
Naming the Goddess is written by over eighty adherents and
scholars of Goddess and Goddess Spirituality.
Paperback: 978-1-78279-476-9 ebook: 978-1-78279-475-2

Shapeshifting into Higher Consciousness
Heal and Transform Yourself and Our World with Ancient
Shamanic and Modern Methods
Llyn Roberts
Ancient and modern methods that you can use every day
to transform yourself and make a positive difference in the
world.
Paperback: 978-1-84694-843-5 ebook: 978-1-84694-844-2

**Readers of ebooks can buy or view any of these
bestsellers by clicking on the live link in the title. Most
titles are published in paperback and as an ebook.
Paperbacks are available in traditional bookshops. Both
print and ebook formats are available online.**

**Find more titles and sign up to our readers' newsletter at
http://www.johnhuntpublishing.com/paganism. Follow
us on Facebook at
https://www.facebook.com/MoonBooks
and Twitter at https://twitter.com/MoonBooksJHP.**